CalmWaters Entertainment Group, Inc.

presents

I0111122

RAGE

Dean Jéan-Pierre

Rage© 2018 by Dean Jéan-Pierre
CalmWaters Entertainment Group, Inc.

Library of Congress Cataloging-in-Publication Data
Dean Jéan-Pierre
ISBN: 978-0-9968835-4-2
This is a work of fiction.

Book Design: Cynthia Colbert
Original Photo By: Malik Williams
"Screaming Malik" on acrylic on canvas, 90 cm X 90 cm, realized in 2007 by Claude Cauquil.

Dean Jéan-Pierre
www.deanjeanpierre.com

Dean Anthony Jéan-Pierre

"To be a Negro in this country and to be relatively conscious is to be in a rage almost all the time."

– James A. Baldwin

RAGE

DEDICATED TO THE PEOPLE OF COLOR who were murdered, simply for being Black, for being Brown, for not being white. I wish I knew every single name of every single slave, in every corner of the world, so I could say their names out loud. A death isn't just the end for that one person, the ramifications are most times unseen; a silent black killer disease and can cripple a family tree. You multiply all these deaths across the generations and the epidemic of dysfunction and lost possibilities is never-ending. I wish I knew the names of every person who suffered from an act of bigotry and intolerance, so I could urge them to not let the small minds of the ignorant set you on a path to defer your dreams. And for those who perpetuated these acts of violence and intolerance, I want to say something deep and meaningful, but all I feel is sadness for someone who could hate another human being, simply because they are different. It is only when you remove yourself from your comfort zone and experience different cultures, you can then see people as they are, human beings just like yourself. Struggling to make their way in this world, without the added weight of having to wonder why another person hates them for simply being from another part of the world or a different ethnicity. Life is difficult enough. Why do we make it so much harder?

Table of Contents

Thank You, Mr. President

Watching you leave me now, feels almost like a breakup. You know it's coming, but when that day finally arrives, it's harder than you ever thought it would be to say goodbye. Boyz II Men had it right. I know I have to let you go, but the selfish part of me wishes you could stay forever and be my President. You are family. A trusted friend. A father figure. We have been together for eight years now and imagining my life without you is unfathomable. I must admit it has made me teary-eyed. Seeing you shed a tear or two a few times has made me want to embrace that side of myself also. Just knowing you were there fighting for me every single day made me feel safe. It made me want to fight harder because everything was against us to succeed, and yet, like our ancestors before us, we willed ourselves to see beyond the day, beyond the moment to a brighter future. Now that it's over, even though I feel sad as I reminisce on the good times (and there were many good times) and the bad times, it fills me with great pride and appreciation to have shared my life with you. In today's society, we put everyone on a pedestal for arbitrary reasons that make no sense. But you, I believe you are deserving because you served as a beacon of hope for millions of people all around the world. You reflected the best of all of us to the world. You showed us what was possible, even against impossible odds. The baton was passed to you and you trudged up that hill with the weight of the world on your shoulders, never wavering and always believing you were on the side of the people, and for that, the people embraced you as their champion.

I am sad, but I am also grateful that because of you, I got a chance to live history instead of reading about it in a dusty book. I still remember the first time I saw you. It was a beautiful fall day in a sleepy little town in Leesburg, Virginia on October 22, 2008. A few of us skipped work that day and drove two hours from Washington, DC just to see you. A crowd of ten thousand was expected, but closer to thirty thousand people showed up that day. You were a rock star who couldn't sing. You were a rock star with your words to move an audience. Your words challenged people to find their better selves. Thirty feet away from you, nestled in a sea of rainbow supporters, I was mesmerized. The wave of emotion surged through the crowd and we chanted your name like a prayer song. We wanted our voices to rise to the heavens as we fervently screamed, *Yes We Can!* The nation answered your call for change and a more inclusive America, not once, but twice. We elected you as our President, the first Black President of the United States of America. Euphoria swept across the land, *the world.* You were not supposed to happen in our lifetime. Men and women wept openly. It finally felt as if we belonged and weren't just guests in a country our ancestors built.

Thank you for governing with grace and dignity.

Thank you for your exemplary family.

Thank you for being scandal free.

Thank you for being respectful and inclusive of all people.

Thank you for never once embarrassing us or abusing the trust placed in you. Thank you for being a strong, Black man.

I hope to one day meet you and shake your hand and just say thank you. As you exit the world stage, but never our hearts, accomplishments are judged by cold, hard numbers. Many will say your accomplishments didn't match your soaring oratory skills and your celebrity status that was thrust upon you. But I would argue that who and what you are mattered more than anything you could have accomplished or made into law. People need symbols. It allows them to hope. It allows them to see themselves beyond their circumstances. It gives them reason to smile. When you smile you want to see another day. You want better for yourself, friends and family. You were the warmth of the sun on our faces because in you we saw our sons, brothers, husbands and fathers. In your wife we saw our sisters, mothers, daughters and wives. You belonged to us because for so long, we were seen as "others and different." In truth, you didn't belong to anyone. The world was your family. Time will give everyone a better perspective and the ability to contrast this new administration with yours. I am certain when that time arrives, there will be a greater appreciation of your accomplishments.

I refuse to say goodbye. Instead I will say, see you soon, President Obama. From a grateful nation, thank you. Obama out.

11.19.16

All Lives Don't Matter

Implicitly all lives matter in a perfect world
It shouldn't have to be said to be understood
If you could step back for a moment,
Take off your rose-colored glasses
Imagine what it feels like to be Black in this country
Take a walk in the shoes of your fellow Black citizens
See the justice system through their skeptical eyes
Knowing there is always a chance history will be repeated
There is a discrepancy in the way Black folks are treated
White folks committing the most heinous crimes
Live to see another day and have their day in court
Black folks by virtue of their skin color never get that chance
You are guilty before you are ever innocent
Gunned down like characters in a video game
Black don't crack but it can be killed and mutilated
Often times it feels like this country has more compassion
For its pets than for its fellow Black Citizens
We are begging to be recognized as equals
Sometimes just as humans
No preferential treatment, just our day in court
Even then the sentences are biased
Where can we get justice in this country?
In the streets, we are gunned down for being Black
In the courts, we are sentenced
For profit and cheap labor for corporate America

Dean Jéan-Pierre

A system of oppression churns out
Black bodies like an assembly line
We are always waiting for the other shoe to drop
Never fully feeling safe in our adopted home
Maybe that's the point of it all to let us know
We brought you here against your will
Damaged you spiritually and mentally
For generations to come
And you will always be
Just a guest and a citizen in name only.

(Listening to *War* by Bob Marley)

Domestic Terrorism

Our sons and daughters
Are being beaten and slaughtered by the police
Our husbands and fathers marginalized in this police state
Our mothers and sisters have cried too many sleepless nights
They too are on the front lines of this fight for our dignity,
For our survival
Domestic terrorism has come home to roost
The fear of times gone by are alive and well in America
A time machine from the past has landed
In this once Beautiful future
We surely aren't living in Wakanda
Plymouth rock is in every yard
There is a palpable fear of being helpless,
Without a voice among the masses
A quiet resolve is slowly brewing
The ones in authority are breaking the laws with impunity
Hiding behind the fear of a Black race they once enslaved
Unarmed, we are murdered
Armed, we are criminals
You cannot defend yourself when you don't make the rules
The game is rigged for the masters of the dominant culture
But our people have always been warriors and survivors
We have come too far
To give up the ground our ancestors fought and died for
We have come too far

Dean Jéan-Pierre

To be quiet and afraid and go silently into that good night
Too much is at stake now for our future generations
It is a war for our dignity and humanity
You will not break our ancestors scream from
Their bloodied graves
Much is expected and demanded from us
Much has been lost through the ugliness of racism and hate
It is a not a fight we went looking for,
But it is one we gladly embrace
Do your small part to further the cause
Years from now when your days are golden and numbered
You are sitting on the front porch
You will know you stood for something special
You did not break.
You stood firm like your ancestors
When the forces of a racist society sought to steal what is
Rightfully yours,
Your dignity and humanity you held strong to the very end.

(Vibing to *Fight the Power* by Public Enemy)

Are You Ready for Some Football?

We love to wrap ourselves in the warmth of nostalgia
Recounting tales of the giants who came before us
We take great pride in telling their heroic tales
Wondering if we would have had that kind of courage
They were ordinary people who took a stand
They placed their life and liberty in constant harm
They faced down certain death
With nothing more than their dignity
They didn't have the cloak
Of the Second Amendment to hide behind
On the battlefields of America's streets
They stood their ground
You marvel at the courage it took
With dogs barking at their heels
Police on horses mowing them down like animals
Restaurants refusing their money
Even though the color was green
Being lynched for merely looking at a white woman
Being called boy as they stood proudly as Black Men
This ugly history makes your blood boil like lava
Everywhere they turned, the odds seemed insurmountable
Death was always lurking around the next corner
And now you are asked to do your part
In today's fight for equality
You are asked as a Black person

Dean Jéan-Pierre

To find out what really matters
From the comfort of your own home
Surrounded by imageries and books on the Black struggle
You are asked to simply turn off the television
Millions of televisions going Black around America
Will bring the football masters to the bargaining table
Collectively, we have the economic power
To throw a Hail Mary
Bring the establishment to their Kaeperknees
There are no dogs nipping at your heels
We are free but still being oppressed daily
Even though we are still in danger,
Racism is subtler than ever
Your voice can be heard loud, Black and proud
When the announcer asks are you ready for some football
Turn your television off
And remember the ones who were murdered
Killed, lynched, raped, dehumanized for being born Black
Their dreams never realized and lives cut short
You have Black skin in the game,
Whispering to you from their graves
They were fighting for their lives
You are worried about a football game
Do you realize how trivial that sounds?
You have eyes of innocent children looking at you to lead
Is your conscience worth the pleasure of a football game?
Are you so easily bought and cannot see the big picture?
You can make as many excuses as you want
So, you can sleep at nights

RAGE

In your participation, you are complicit
And holding hands with this corrupt system
The fact remains you care more for a game
Than you do for your own people
You cannot stand on the sidelines
Waiting for things to change
Imagine if our ancestors had done what you are doing
We would still be slaves
Waiting for someone to come save us
No one is coming to save us; we have to save ourselves
It starts with a simple gesture
By telling the NFL that BLM more than a national anthem.

(Listening to *Oh Freedom* by The Golden Gospel Singers)

Dean Jéan-Pierre

Mountaintop

You can beat my body
You can deny me my inalienable rights as a human being
You can try all these things in the name of being American
You can even call yourself a Christian
When you sleep at night and you pray to your God
The same God I pray to every night
You tell him how your day went
How much you love your country, wife and children
How much you bleed red, white and blue
It's the only color you truly care about
My Black skin has no value to you
It is only valued in servitude to exploit
You can claim to understand my plight, but how could you
Your children have never been murdered,
Simply for being Black
Your women raped and disposed of without a conscience,
Simply for being Black
Your men beaten into submission and lynched,
Simply for being Black
You know nothing of true pain and suffering
Suffering so horrific
We have prayed for the sweet release of death
But even in death we cannot rest in peace
We find some way to keep moving forward
It is what we do as Black folks
Suffering can drown you in pain

RAGE

Leaving you too angry to move forward
We find hope in the next generation
That they will break the ceiling and reach for the sky
Bringing with them
Every disenfranchised and forgotten soul
To enjoy the view from the mountaintop
That Dr. King so eloquently spoke about.

(Vibing to *Strange Fruit* by Nina Simone)

Dean Jéan-Pierre

Black Face

You are just another dead Black face on the evening news
Barely human enough to warrant sympathy
Before moving on to more important stories
Animals are regarded higher than us
If they were being slaughtered
As we are in the streets of America
The outrage of white society would be swift and united
Cries and protests of being inhumane would be heard
But for us there is cautious indifference
A collective sigh of not believing,
This still happens in America
It happens every day, captured on video for posterity
Still not believed because we are the reason for own demise
Shared and deciphered on social media
Everyone has an opinion
No one has a solution
Another one will come along to grab our attention
Our rage will pass because we are being conditioned
Violence becomes acceptable
It leads the news on every channel
To be silent is to be complicit
And yet you remain on the sidelines, waiting
Showing more compassion for animals
Instead of your fellow man
The Black Life is devalued beginning at birth
We have to find our own worth in this life

RAGE

Even as society views it as expendable
Another dead Black face on the evening news
What did they do this time to cause their demise
Is always the unsaid question
Before moving on to something more important.

(Listening to *Changes* by Tupac)

Dean Jéan-Pierre

Maybe

And I wonder sometimes
About bringing another Black life into this world
Knowing the truth about the adversities they will face
A young child already labeled a criminal

Already assumed to be inferior
Destined to fail in society's eyes
Even before their potential is fully realized
They are criminalized
And placed on the assembly line for profit
Am I being selfish by playing God
Maybe in their lifetime a cure will be found
Maybe racism will be a foreign concept
Unable to be conjured by a new generation
Maybe a pill can cure all this hatred
Maybe our children can just be children
Free to believe everything is possible
Maybe our women can just be women
Free to be themselves without that extra burden
Maybe our men can just be men
They can exhale and embrace their Blackness
Maybe all we imagined this country can be
Will one day come to pass
Until that time arrives,
I will keep looking for racism around every corner.

(Vibing to *Black Butterfly* by Deniece Williams)

You Wonder Why

And you wonder why we are distrustful of your intentions
How many times have you used our Black bodies for profit
How many times have you smiled in our faces
And done us harm
How many of our women have you raped
How many of our men have you murdered
And you wonder why there are no fathers at home
The scoreboard of oppression is too long to count
Even after all that, we are still a people who forgive
We pray to the same God who protects you
But somehow the bounty on our heads is neverending
It's a question I hope to ask God one day
Why were we forsaken and brutalized for generations
It's an answer with which I will have to respectfully disagree
When I remember all the Black bodies
That have been burned, beaten, raped, lynched, spat upon,
And treated worse than a wild animal
Someone has to answer for that,
Whoever that someone might be.

(Vibing to *What's Going On* by Marvin Gaye)

Dean Jéan-Pierre

Water Fountain

You don't want us on your golf courses
You don't want us drinking your coffee
Just asking for utensils is a criminal offense
You can keep your fucking apology
It comes from a disingenuous place
We need to keep our money in our communities
We know how you really feel about us
You would rather we stay on our side of the town
Pretend that we don't exist but those days are long gone
You want us to drink from our own water fountains
Use our own segregated bathrooms
You know, like the good old days
I would rather know my enemy hates my Black ass
Than for you to smile in my face
With a noose behind your back and a lie on your lips
You love our foods, all spicy
Even though you don't want us in your country
A country you stole as you claim to make it great again
Great for your ancestors but mine would say differently
We are good enough to babysit your kids
Back in the day pink lips sucked on Big Momma's nipples
Bounced on her lap joyously
While her own kids sometimes went hungry
You take our recipes and Columbus that shit up
There is nothing new about collard greens
Just gentrification with a new label

RAGE

Taking credit for something you did not discover
Like Rock n' Roll being whitewashed from its true creators
You feel emboldened now like never before
You can remove your sheet to show your true color
One of your own is in the White House
Looking like one of the slave masters
Spouting rhetoric about making America great again
We won't allow the progress made to be forgotten
We have come too far to ever go back to picking cotton.

(Listening to *Story of OJ* by Jay Z)

Dean Jéan-Pierre

Fishbowl

I am the son of parents who love me
I am a father to children I vow to always protect
I am a husband to a wife I simply adore
I am a friend to others who look like me
I am all of these people before I am Black
Before you see my existence as just a color
Or judge me by viral hash-tagged media stereotypes
Imagine for a minute what it's like to be me
To walk in Black skin viewed as a constant threat
To always be aware that you are being watched
To change who you are to acquiesce
Even as an individual
You are expected to represent your entire race
Can you imagine the pressure not to crack?
Constantly swimming in a fishbowl like salmon upstream
I am not asking for special treatment
I am not asking to pass as one of you
Treat me as what I am, a man before a color.

(Listening to *F.U.B.U* by Solange)

Hash Tag Life

My son turns to me for answers
We share the same emotions but I cannot show mine
I must remain strong, even though I am scared to death
I must remain hopeful even though I am drowning in grief
Another Black man murdered by police
His life reduced to a hash tag, a slogan to go viral
Black Lives Matter should be a foregone conclusion
His past indiscretions debated on television
Trying to find a reason that makes sense
An excuse to make his murder legal
His past wasn't known in that deadly moment
Only the color of his skin was his judge and jury
A man cannot rest in peace
When his last image is one of violence
His spirit will forever be restless, searching for answers
The same answers my son needs to continue believing
That the same thing won't happen to him,
His friends or his father
I see the fear in his eyes, even as he tries to remain strong
He is following my lead, looking to me for answers
This time I have none; I only have anger
I hug my son so he cannot see my tears falling
Another Black Man killed for no damn good reason.

(Listening to *Blackman Redemption* by Bob Marley)

Dean Jéan-Pierre

Coffee Makes It Better

Your forefathers were my masters
You owned my people like cattle
Now we sit together as friends
Laughing over expensive coffee at Starbucks
Discussing cinema and poetry
Arguing over politics and religion
The absurdity of what once was is a fleeting thought
One human owning another human
How is that even possible that it could ever happen
There is sometimes an uneasy silence between us
A deeper conversation of race and privilege is needed
Mixed in with politics, literary and music would be nice
It's much too beautiful a day for a topic so ugly and divisive
So we continue our roles as actors in this tragic comedy
Over a sip of coffee, three sugars no milk for me
I like my coffee Black, no dilution.

(Listening to *A Change Is Gonna Come* by Donny Hathaway)

Fear

You fear my color not me
You see stereotypes
And not a human being
I should not have to make you comfortable
To be seen, respected
The same courtesy I extend to you
Only goes one way.

(Listening to *Black Man* by Stevie Wonder)

Dean Jéan-Pierre

Reality

I am not fearful when driving
I am just more cautious than necessary
I am not fearful in a new neighborhood
I am just more aware than I should have to be
I am not fearful when walking behind a white woman
I just make sure not to walk too closely
I keep my hands out of my pockets
No sudden movements just in case
It is not something I was taught
It is just my survivor's instinct kicking in unconsciously
I am not fearful and, yet, I am not myself.

(Listening to *Fear of a Black Planet* by Public Enemy)

Blood Nation

Sunrise wakes me up this morning
Already feeling the weight of the world on my shoulders
I keep the news turned off
Say a prayer before hopping out of bed
I just cannot take any more death right now
Another Black man shot down like a dog in the street
More excuses of noncompliance
More reasons to exterminate us legally
History is slowly being repeated
A police state is slowly coming to fruition
Mass incarceration is the law of the land
Peaceful resistance is met
With guns and bullets, angry rhetoric
This time we cannot turn the other cheek
Prayer will not save us
God will not stop this hatred of our Black skin
A nation born of blood
Can only be reborn in that same blood.

(Listening to *911 Is A Joke* by Public Enemy)

Dean Jéan-Pierre

Scriptures of Forgiveness

Even as I bow my head in prayer
The world we live in I just don't understand anymore
Even as I ask you to forgive those who are evil
A quiet part of me
Wants them to pay for their sins here on Earth
A part of me
Wants them to suffer like the innocent lives they have taken
But I know it is not the way of Scriptures

Please forgive me Father, I humbly pray
I am only human and vengeance is not mine to seek
Evil cannot ever be understood
To understand would require empathy
All we can do is be vigilant and look out for our neighbors
Evil only prospers when good people do nothing
So even as the assault against my Blackness continues
The belief that good triumphs over evil still reigns supreme
There seems to be less evidence of this than ever before
Without that hope then all is lost
That is the lesson amongst all this sadness
Goodness and life has to be treasured
It is the only path for humanity to continue its survival
For this I pray. Amen.

(Listening to *U Will Know* by Black Men United)

Serena

When what was created naturally is no longer valued
When the standard of beauty does not fit a certain description
Everything else is viewed as less than to sell a narrative
The rainbow is filled with many beautiful colors
The challenge becomes being inclusive
When it is something that should just come naturally
Beauty by definition is subjective
Viewed through a prism of an already narrow focus
Anything else that doesn't fit the societal norm
Is met with indifference
New terminology to create separate but equal,
Like not Classically beautiful becomes in fashion
The not so subtle undermining of a culture continues to persist
The femininity of our women is always being called into question
As if our beauty is some dark forbidden mystery
As if Webster's definition is meant for only one race
What is this need to constantly try and tear us down?
A futile attempt to keep us in our place
Our place is anywhere we want to be
We are just as beautiful as you, no less or no more
There is a rainbow of beauty to discover beyond your own
Open your prism of supposed beauty superiority
And recognize that Black is beautiful too.

(Listening to *Brown Skin* by India.Arie)

Dean Jéan-Pierre

Nameless Cloud

There is a cloud over my people
I don't want to call it Black
It feels like a plague
A constant dark passenger
Stealing away our breaths
With an elbow pressed against our necks
Cloaking us in pain
As we pray religiously to a merciful God
A god who hasn't balanced the scales
Maybe in the afterlife our suffering will be rewarded
Maybe then we can ask why were we forsaken
Were we the bastard children easily discarded
Maybe then we will get answers
I hope I am not still angry and filled with rage.

(Listening to *Don't Shoot* by The Game)

Hallowed Halls

If you listen quietly enough
If you close your eyes
You can hear their voices
You can feel their laughter
Hear their cries
You can feel their pain
You can feel their struggle
The hardships endured
The prayers unanswered
They were seen as property
Stripped of their humanity
Their eyes were turned to the future
Knowing with every life lost
Every dream buried
Every family torn apart their lives still had meaning
Their deaths would serve to inspire
The generation to come after
Here you are today living the lives they dreamed
Everything is far from perfect
There are still obstacles to overcome
Somewhere the ghost of your ancestors is smiling
Taking solace in the life you are living
A life they couldn't even dream possible
You are the dream, the hope of a generation deprived
You walk in their hallowed steps

Dean Jéan-Pierre

Taking them places once forbidden and illegal
It is not a burden to go forth with that history always present
It is a privilege and an honor you should always respect.

(Listening to *Immigrant* by Sade)

Words Matter

And I know it's now a term of endearment
It was once used to dehumanize us
We were treated worse than animals
But worked twice as hard as cattle
I cringe with embarrassment
When I hear it spoken by our children
When I hear it tossed around casually in conversation
They know not the history of its origin
But what is your excuse as an adult
You glorify a word
Used as a weapon of hate against your ancestors
Burned into their skin and deeper into their conscience
Whipped on their bloodied backs embedded like a tattoo
Spat with hate to their face
And now you use it as a greeting, a term of endearment
Maybe your argument would hold true
When you say you are taking away its power
There are other words readily available
That are far less hateful
The history of a word used for over four hundred years
Cannot be cleansed as if it never existed
Your soul should cry rivers of tears
Every time that word is uttered from your mouth
The souls of our ancestors should rise up in umbrage
That their pain is now being used for profit

Dean Jéan-Pierre

Some words matter
They carry a history of a people denied their basic humanity
Even now their story is being whitewashed
Gentrified to ease a nation's guilty conscience
It is an insult to their memory and the legacy of slavery
When we allow such ugly words to be spoken so casually
One would think maybe it was all a dream.

(Listening to *Be Free: Stop Killing Our People* by J. Cole)

Rage

My screams echo shell shocked in my thoughts
Each one reverberating like a gunshot blasting through hope
Hope lays at my feet, taking its last dying breath
My Rage feels like a bomb strapped to my chest
Ready to explode at the slightest provocation
Black Officer shoots white woman, indicted
White Officer shoots Black man, no charges filed
His defense is he was in fear for his life
If he was in fear, imagine how we feel without a gun
Without the law on our side
Even amongst the rank and file, a Black life is worthless
I wrap my arms around my chest
Searching for a memory to disintegrate my Rage
Too many times now, we pray for answers
Too many times now, it feels like no one is listening
A Rage this deep trembles in my shackled bones
It runs hot and angry through my blood
We've been marching for years for justice for our loved ones
Lady Justice remains blindfolded ignoring our pain
This Rage I feel building will soon detonate
Even though I feel justified to seek vengeance
The outcome of a life of violence is either death or the penitentiary
Either way, I lose in this real life version of Catch 22.

(Listening to *Don't Believe the Hype* by Public Enemy)

Dean Jéan–Pierre

Kumbaya

You put your hands on her
You put your hands on me
You put your hands on us
There will be a price to be paid
A reckoning with the force of all our anger
Fire summoned from countless graves
Too many voices silenced
Too many cries never heard
We will not turn the other cheek
We did that once before
No mercy will be shown
Kumbaya is our dead ancestors slaughtered and murdered
The fire this time
The chickens have come home to roost
We shall stand our ground
We shall make our ancestors proud
They paid the ultimate price for our freedom
The least we can do is fight to keep it.

(Listening to *Soldier* by Erykah Badu)

Freed Slave

My debt to society has been paid in full
Even though it's a debt I didn't earn
I am free now but it still feels like jail
You want every pound of my Black flesh
You want to beat me into submission until I scream Massa
Only then will you be satisfied
To see me reduced as a human being
You had my body locked in a cage
My mind was free to fly to keep me sane
My imagination you could never own
On the outside now I am a marked man, still a felon
Unworthy of a second chance
My record makes me unhireable
Even menial labor is seen as too good for me
How is a man supposed to make a living
And regain his dignity
If he can't find a job to feed his family
To hold his head high after doing his nine-to-five
A second chance should come with a clean slate
The right to vote should be restored
Putting him in charge of his destiny
You don't want me empowered
You don't want me standing tall
You need me on my knees, bended
I will not beg for what is rightfully mine

47

Dean Jéan-Pierre

I will not break because I know my worth
My mind is free even though my body is enslaved
In a society that does not recognize my humanity.

(Listening to *If I Ruled The World* by Nas & Lauryn Hill)

The Resistance

Dig deep, find the courage to resist
Your voice is your weapon of choice
But when the time comes to defend yourself,
Do not hesitate
Raised fists are still fists
A loud voice can still rally a nation
Your life is just as precious as theirs
The second amendment guarantees you that right
Even though it was enacted without us in mind
Beyond a law,
You have the sovereign right as a human being
To defend your person
From all those who seek to do you harm
Do no turn the other cheek
You will be left defenseless
Do not fall for the smile and the handshake
While your culture is being plundered for profit
Remember who you are
Remember what you have lost
Remember what is at stake
Black and proud
Is more than just a slogan
The revolution will be televised
And is more than just a commercial.

(Listening to *Baltimore* by Prince)

Dean Jéan–Pierre

Human on Human Crime

I wish all our tears could heal all this hate
I wish all our prayers could save some lives
Wishing is a prayer that is never answered
We continue to be murdered by those sworn to protect us
We continue to kill our brothers with our own Black hands
Is one death worse than the other?
Is there more value in being killed by your brother?
The world is broken
Humanity has lost its way
My brother is not your brother
My values are not your values
If we saw each other as simply human beings
Not a color, a religion or a threat to our person
Maybe then we could start a conversation
Maybe the next generation could get it right
Blood will continue to flow religiously
Mothers will continue to bury their sons and husbands
Change requires actions not words
To look ourselves in the mirror
Is to see God and the Devil running side by side
For the souls of a country still in turmoil.

(Listening to *The Women Gather* by Sweet Honey in the Rock)

Don't Call It A Comeback

Once upon a time we were called Niggers
Some of us were called mulattos and Jigaboos
Years passed and we came up in the world
We were called Colored but it still meant the same thing
Just a nicer name still filled with hate for us
Something happened in the Sixties and the pride we felt
Manifested into us being called Black
Black was beautiful
Black was strong
Black didn't take no mess
Black was Proud
Now we are called African-Americans
I am still not sure what that really means
Hyphenated to give us roots
A connection to the Motherland most of us will never visit
Some of us still prefer Black
Black has an identity, roots that cannot be destroyed
More and more these days
It doesn't matter what we are called
History is repeating itself
Nigger once whispered behind closed doors
Once felt in the stares and dirty looks of intolerance
Has been dusted off and polite company is now emboldened
To say that hateful word
Gifted in a smile of false camaraderie

Dean Jéan-Pierre

A term once buried with all its murdered victims
Is back in vogue and resurrected
The past has come back for a visit
To reclaim its ugly history with a vengeance
Don't call it a comeback,
It's always been here
Just waiting for its army to regain strength
With us as their willing accomplice.

(Listening to *Letter To The Free* by Common)

Open Season

Put your hands up
Keep your hands down
Comply with the officer's warning
Challenge a direct command
Walk away
Run away
Stand your ground
Be an honor student
Be a thug on the street
College-educated
GED in your hip pocket
Dressed professionally for corporate America
Pants sagging, no belt, underwear showing
Man, woman, child
All hues of Black and Brown
Keep a smile on your face
Keep your voice pleasant
Be that angry Black person
Be peaceful and loving
Come from a one-parent household
Be rich and famous
Raise the bass until thunder roars
None of that matters
Only one profile matters
The dark hue of your skin makes you a target

Dean Jéan-Pierre

No one is safe
It is open season in the land of the free
Home of the brave on citizens still viewed as lesser than
In a country that preaches equality
Ironically invades other countries
To bring justice and liberation
While at home, its citizens
Are being gunned down with impunity
A country founded in blood, can only be reborn in blood.

(Listening to *Sound of Da Police* by KRS-One)

Mind Your Manners

We are raised to mind our manners
Be respectful of all adults
Say our prayers, God will answer
Have blind faith, he is always watching
We are told go to school, get an education
Get married and raise a family
When you can, give back to the community
Be a good citizen, a credit to your race
Somewhere in there, find time to be happy
You do all these things to the best of your abilities
Then one day you might turn down the wrong street
End up in the wrong neighborhood, whatever that means
Driving a car that's a bit too fancy, whatever that means
You might fit the profile of someone Black
And on that day
Everything you have done in your life doesn't matter
You are reduced to every stereotype associated with us
Your life hangs in the balance and has come to this moment
The slightest unintended provocation
And you become another statistic
Unarmed Black man killed by the police
More outrage on social media
Crying mothers on the evening news
Protests and marches in the community
The one with all the power claims he was in fear for his life

Dean Jéan-Pierre

Being Black seems to be more dangerous than being armed
A Black life shouldn't be so easily disposed
Discarded at the whim of a gun and badge
By someone who stands in judgment, who has no conscience
Maybe it's time we stopped minding our manners
Take a look at the man in the mirror
Maybe it's time we started fighting for our lives
Maybe it's time we listen to Malcolm
Maybe it's time we inhabit the spirit of the Black Panther
Not the one who hails from Wakanda.

(Listening to *Man in the Mirror* by Michael Jackson)
(The King of It All)

False Narrative

You don't know me as a person
You judge me by what you see on television
Negative imagery encapsulated in snippets
Beamed and repackaged to millions of Fox-fed viewers
Sold as absolute truth for profit
I have the same hopes and dreams as your children
You don't live the American Dream in my Black skin
You don't understand how angry it makes me
Seeing my people constantly disrespected and marginalized
It consumes my mind in hopes of a solution
There is a secret answer somewhere we haven't yet found
But until America confronts its past and present
Its citizens will continue to live in denial
Denial fostered by a false narrative
Viewed through the lens of supposed superiority
It has always been an unfair race
The decks constantly stacked and repackaged
The line is moved and reimagined
And yet, it is never enough for those who have stolen our heritage
It is never enough to keep our men incarcerated
They will not stop until they make this country great again
Great for who?
It was never great for us
Even now as we prosper more than our ancestors
We are still fighting some of the same fights, just better disguised

Dean Jéan-Pierre

We cannot afford to be tired
There is still so much work left to be done.

(Listening to *Zombie* by Fela Kuti)

Still Traveling

If you saw me as a person
Someone equal; someone human
Someone who is loved; someone with a family
Someone who has hopes and dreams
Someone just as worthy as you to be alive
Someone who is an American
Maybe then you would think twice before using violence to defuse
Instead of words to understand
Compassion to walk in my shoes
Entitlement to defend the indefensible
The path that brought us here to a foreign land we now call home
Often times we are made to feel like visitors
A tenant without rights; a guest without a country
You want to forget the history of your violence
I would want to forget, too, if I were you
I want to always remember how my people suffered
It keeps me hungry, inspired
I don't do it for the culture
I do it for the ones who never had the opportunity to prosper
I do it with the hope that one day in the future,
The old Negro spiritual, We Shall Overcome
Will one day be obsolete and we will have finally arrived.

(Listening to *On & On* by Erykah Badu)

Dean Jéan-Pierre

Roots

What is it about my hair that makes you so uncomfortable
Do you believe wearing it natural
Makes me more in touch with my roots
Do you have flashbacks of my ancestors
When you see me in my natural state of Blackness
Kinky, Black, unapologetic and proud
Unwilling to be compromised for your comfort
The fire next time is upon us
A revolution is fast approaching on the horizon
The chickens are hungry in the garden
And playing nice with the roosters
They want to be fed by any means necessary
Does my locs and braids remind you of whips and chains
Does it give you pause when you recall the past
Sins of atrocities whisper in your ear
You feel a fear you don't recognize
Your great, great-grandparents owned mine
They gave me their name and stole my history
You don't have to apologize but at least empathize
Your clan ascended on the whipped backs of my people
Taking credit for work you didn't perform
And you call my Black people lazy
My ancestors worked and sweated hard enough
Every Black person should be on vacation for eternity
You want to strip me of my history
Leave me ignorant and dependent on your charity

RAGE

While asking me to forget your brutality
When you haven't even yet asked for my forgiveness
I would not grant you mercy
The roots of my ancestors are planted in the soil of this country
Enriched with their spilled blood
Fertilized with their stolen sweat
Not a day goes by I will ever forget.

(Listening to *Don't Touch My Hair* by Solange)

Dean Jéan-Pierre

Kaepernick

Kaepernick takes a knee
White America goes ballistic with anger
The visual of a Black man standing up for himself
By ironically kneeling peacefully in silence
Ruffles the chains long buried and slowly awakening
But another Black man gets murdered by the police
Their outrage turns to silence and indifference
The fault must lay in us
Because we are prone to criminal behavior
It's a lynch mob mentality to a faulty conclusion
Our dissent does not make us un-American or less patriotic
But if you only see us as Black, African-American,
And that other word but not American
You can excuse our protest
As something trivial or retribution
You can muddy the waters with cries of patriotism
While the insidious disease of racism
Marches across this land
Its army of hate is getting stronger by the day
The land of red, white and blue
Where only one color matters
Someone screams all lives matter,
Even comedians know it's a joke
For a country that has so much to offer
A country that is held up as a beacon of light
To the rest of the world

RAGE

Its unwillingness to shine a light on its darkest shame
To take ownership of its greatest sin
Hoping it will all somehow all magically disappear
And somehow make America great again
Greatness cannot be attained
When a segment of your population is disenfranchised
When they are being brutalized without just cause
It's modern day slavery
And the streets of America is the new plantation
The police sworn to protect are the new Massas
Using their guns as whips and chains to keep us in line
We have been down this road before,
Too much ground has been gained
Too much blood has been spilled
Even on bended knees,
Our fists are raised to the sky
The fire this time.

(Listening to *To Be Young, Gifted and Black* by Donny Hathaway)

Dean Jéan-Pierre

Marginalized

The tide of anger rises in my chest
Dangerously close to drowning my common sense
There comes a point of no return
When you have been marginalized for far too long
You want to be seen
You want to be respected as a human being
You want the world to know you are not invisible
Who you are matters beyond your race
Your life has value even when it is not protected
Loved ones wait for you on your side of town
Knowing that any day could be your last
Mothers should not have to fear for the safety of their children
From those sworn to protect them
Fathers should not have to be strong to be a man
When the seed of anger has taken root slowly turning to hatred
Everything becomes colored by race
The humanity of who we are is forgotten
It becomes us against them and the noise gets louder
No one is listening
Everyone is right
No one is wrong
The world is fractured and in need of healing
We sing for peace in the voices of our ancestors
We march for our children as they did for us
The struggle continues
As we ask humans to treat other humans with respect

RAGE

We have been marginalized for far too long
We have miles to go still, but the sun is slowly setting
Things have gotten better, but better is still not good enough.

(Listening to *A Change Is Gonna Come* by Sam Cooke)

Dean Jéan-Pierre

White Rage

Misplaced anger
You vote against your own self-interests
Programs designed to help the disenfranchised
And because it was a championed by a Black Man as President
You turned your back on much needed help
You look at Black people as being less than
Even though your struggles are the same
Your oppressor lurks in the shadows smiling
He looks just like you, while he points a finger at me
Whispering in your ear I am the boogie man,
Coming to steal your woman
Coming to take jobs you don't even want
Your fear is irrational but rooted in hatred
The same things you have done to us for generations
You fear will be done to you with equal violence
I am not here to assuage your guilty conscience
Too many of my people who are innocent are dying
Your oppressor has pulled the ultimate con,
Playing to your biases and insecurities
He knows how to exploit your fears to keep him in his castle
He tells you to blame the Black man
Who has no power except his voice
While he hoards all of his power
And laughs at how gullible and stupid you are
Once upon a time he would hide in the shadows
Pulling the strings

RAGE

Now you are so blinded by hatred
He can hide in plain sight in his white mask
Go about his business and watch you do his work
While you shout out meaningless slogans about being great again
Not all nostalgia is wrapped up in good memories
We still wear the scars of this racist country
Our backs might be healed
But our souls are still crying for all the ones we have lost
They will never have their day of justice in court.

(Listening to *They Don't Care About Us* by Michael Jackson)
(The King of It All)

Dean Jéan-Pierre

Criminalizing Blackness

At least if I had a gun in my hand to defend my life
At least then,
You feared for your life excuse would be a plausible defense
A bag of Skittles can get you killed
Sitting and waiting in a Starbucks will get you arrested
Knocking on a door asking for help can get you shot
A wallet mistaken for a gun can get you murdered
Carrying a legal weapon with a permit still makes you a target
Selling cigarettes gets you choked out because you can't breathe
A cellphone is now a lethal weapon in the hands of a Black Man
The truth is, it wouldn't matter
You would still be murdered
Your only crime is being Black in America
We send our children out in the world with words and prayers
The enemy is armed with guns and the justice system
How are they supposed to survive such odds
Prayer and good manners won't save them
We are setting them up for failure
But the choices are limited in this encounter
When someone in power wants you dead
When they view your life as expendable, easily disposable
How are you supposed to get home to your family alive
Blackness has been criminalized in this country
With euphemistic language
Dog whistle words and imagery to rile up
A segment of the population

RAGE

They fondly remember
How things were for their grandparents' generation
They never consider how life was for mine
That's the problem with privilege
You never see the other side
Not because you can't
It's just because you don't want to.

(Listening to *Brotha* by Angie Stone)

Dean Jéan-Pierre

Colonizer

If you had to live in my Black skin
Experience my American terror in living color
Maybe then you wouldn't be so quick to dismiss my anger
You wouldn't be so quick to tell me to get over it
Maybe then you would understand
Why reparations are in order
Even then that would not be enough for all that has been lost
Maybe then you wouldn't want to own
A share of the word Nigger
A word that has been white-washed
By those with Black faces
By those spitting rhymes for profit
As your silent co-conspirators
They claim they are doing it for the culture
They are doing it for the dollars
You displaced an entire culture
Who wasn't in need of a white savior, a colonizer
You placed them in bondage for generations
Mentally, physically and spiritually
And, now you admonish me to take responsibility for my life
While you still haven't
Owned up for your centuries of crimes
If you lived in my Black skin and felt the depths of my pain
Growing roots so deep in my blood
Sometimes I can't even breathe
It leaves me gasping for air

RAGE

You would hate yourself for all the suffering you have caused
Appropriation and Gentrification
Are the new hashtags for our rage
You have equity in the sins committed
Like your forefathers before you
You still have Black skin in the game even as you pretend
The world is equal
Balance has been restored
We are now post-racial
If you lived in my Black skin
You would know that America still sometimes feels the same.

(Vibing to *Say It Loud I'm Black and I'm Proud* by James Brown)

Dean Jéan–Pierre

Angry Black Man

They tell me don't be the angry Black Man
Keep a smile on your face
Remain civil in the presence of polite company
There is too much at stake besides your pride
You have to channel your inner minstrel
This is America
You don't want to scare the nice white people
It will only open the curtain behind the mask
Give them a peek into what you're really feeling
A rage so deep if you ever unleashed its ferocity
Spoke the truth in the voice of your dead ancestors
The pain of so many injustices
Combined in one loud scream of rage across generations
It would bring the world to a standstill
It would move Heaven to action
Maybe God's will shall finally be done
I don't want to be the angry Black Man
Even though sometimes it is necessary
Anger is a weight leading to an early grave
Everywhere I turn it feels as if we are in a time machine
The present feels like the past
The future doesn't seem as hopeful
I am waiting for the dogs to be unleashed again
For hatred to darken the sky
Even in the face of evil we must remain vigilant
We must channel our rage in action

RAGE

There is a mind game being played
Just being the angry Black Man isn't enough
You have to play chess with these racist mother*ckers
Checkmate their privilege
Let them know you won't take no shit
We have eaten shit for far too long
It's time we ate a delicious meal at our own table
Be carefree and not have to worry about the bill.

(Vibing to *Inner City Blues-Make Me Wanna Holla*
by Marvin Gaye)

Dean Jéan-Pierre

Sick 'n Tired

We been praying to Jesus for many moons now
Waded through many rivers and waters
The sun has done set on so many innocent souls
Don't you wonder sometimes if Jesus be listening
Or is he somewhere on vacation and we been forgotten
Maybe his Daddy can tell him we need his help
The brown ones who supposedly look like him
We need the blessings of our many prayers
We sick 'n tired of fighting for our dignity
We sick 'n tired of praying for his mercy
We ain't asking for more than what we deserve
Seems like the whole pie done been eaten and ain't none left
The table's been set and we still standing waiting for scraps
Lord knows we ain't a greedy people
We been making due with what little we have, all these years
It would be nice just once to know you see us suffering
We just want to eat what everybody else is eating
Instead of being in the kitchen cooking.

(Vibing to *Sinnerman* by Nina Simone)

OkeyDokey

The decks are stacked
Cards constantly reshuffled
The dealer is crooked
Dealing from the bottom up
Selling you dreams on a deferred payment plan
Written on a bounced check you can never cash
The goal line has moved again
Thought we were catching up,
Moving on up
The elevator is always broken
We are still taking the stairs
We can't catch our breath
Always running, trying to prove ourselves
The okeydokey, another sleight of hand
Playing magician with our lives and dreams
We pay taxes
Use proper English
Sometimes forgetting who we are
As we scramble to get a seat at the table
The American dream is so close, yet so far
Fading slowly over the horizon
A last glimpse of a rainbow filled with so many beautiful colors
Twice as good isn't good enough
When the gatekeepers are always changing the rules.

(Listening to *Glory* by John Legend & Common)

Dean Jéan-Pierre

Good Cops

I keep hearing about all these good cops
I don't doubt for a minute that this is true
The police are always asking the public to come forward
When they see a crime being committed
Yet, they won't do the same
Where are all these good cops I keep hearing about
When my brothers and sisters are being beaten black and blue
By the men in blue sworn to protect and uphold the law
When are these good cops going to step forward
When their brothers in blue have gone over the line
Terrorizing the innocent in the name of vigilante justice
They have no fear of retribution
They are above the law,
Protected by judges in black robes doling out white justice
They know there is a code of silence
Cowboy style justice
Terrorism is not just overseas
It was born and bred right here in the good ole US of A
Silence is consent
Silence makes you complicit
Blood is on your hands
Your finger is on the trigger
You don't see us as human beings
Just another nigger to toss out with the garbage
I have never seen a good cop
Stop his brother from brutalizing one of us

RAGE

It becomes a game of piñata
Who can spill the most blood by cracking a Black skull open
Their batons become whips
Their bullets laced with anger
At perceived slights of being displaced, marginalized
Ain't that funny?
White people worried about
Something we have been living for generations
Where have all the good cops gone
A Black nation wonders and there is just silence.

(Listening to *Get Up, Stand Up* by Bob Marley & The Wailers)

Dean Jéan-Pierre

Strangers on Planet Earth

You clutch your purse when you see me coming
Give me that fake ass smile filled with a warning
I pretend not to see your fear
I am used to white women scared of the big Black man
Our eyes never even meet
You have branded me a criminal because of my Black skin
Dismissed me as a fellow human deserving of respect
You value your purse more than my life
You will march for PETA but BLM doesn't matter
We are strangers on Planet Earth
We live in a vacuum with no communication
Voices are playing but no one is listening
Why are you the one always so fearful
When I am the one always in danger of losing my life
Anything I do can be criminalized
I am at the mercy of your discretion
Not to invoke your white privilege
When the cops come, guns a blazing
They are judge and jury, the final decision
Your white skin will protect you and keep you alive
My Black skin will be judged as a crime
Innocence rewarded with an early grave
Truth rooted in American history of slavery
It makes me so angry that my place in society
Even though guaranteed by law
It always comes with a price to be paid

RAGE

A constant bounty on our heads
Where is your guilty conscience
You oppose reparations but you support gentrification
You scream all lives matter
Now that Black lives matter has become a thing
You need the attention
You feel neglected
We are always at an impasse
Because you have never valued my life
In the way you value yours and your four-legged companions.

(Listening to *I Am That I Am* by Peter Tosh)

Dean Jéan-Pierre

More Rage

This feeling courses through my veins
Like an opioid that is better than crack
A drug we now care about
Because white folks are dying like niggers in the streets
Now it is a national emergency that needs our attention
No one cared when Black folks were hooked on crack
Laws were passed to criminalize us
Now, the government is giving out hugs and free love
This feeling is like a countdown
To a bomb detonation blinding me with rage
It is how I feel every day now
As I make my way through the world
In the wrong hands, a rage like this can end lives
Maybe an innocent life extinguished before it blooms
So I use my rage as fuel to express my thoughts
To cool down the temperature before irrational becomes the norm
Rage without direction is just useless anger
Rage without an objective can be manipulated by others
It can become just as deadly as a bullet
There are millions of others out there, just like me
Going about our lives quietly
We see our Black Skin being used for target practice
Our Black celebrities cooning for the cameras on social media
We are leaderless in a time of great divide
Where is that great Black voice to speak truth to power
Where are today's Malcolm, Martin and Sojourner

RAGE

Everything we fought for in the Sixties, does it still matter
I look around the landscape of society
There are rumblings of a great civil unrest on the horizon
Too long have we been taken for granted
Too long have we been regarded as second-class citizens
You cannot keep taking from those who have nothing
Soon they will have nothing left to lose and rise up
When they rise, this motherfucker might come crashing down
A society built on the blood of slaves
Will soon perish from all its sins unpaid.

(Listening to *Strange Fruit* by Billie Holiday)

Dean Jéan-Pierre

Kanye
(Wake Up Mr. West, Mr. West)

When you done moved on up and left your past behind
You pretend you don't remember the struggle
You're on some artist shit now
And the Black struggle is an inconvenience
Wherever you go in this world
You are a Black man before you're human
Wealth won't save you from being called that name
The one you rap so eloquently about
And now claim as you jet to Paris
Now that you've married the slave master's daughter
No matter how many times you proclaim you're a genius
A gift given is in service to others
You are only serving your own agenda
You are squandering your time on stage
God gave you a platform to affect change
Instead you allow your ego to write your narrative
You allow yourself to be used by the agents of hate
And yet you claim to be provocative
Geniuses don't need reassurance
They just go out and create
Maybe Jay Z had it right
You will always need a mentor because you're not a leader
Where is that dude from College Dropout
The dude that spit with such uncommon passion

RAGE

You couldn't help but root for his success
This person you've become looks lost in the sunken place
Maybe you need a hug, maybe you need love
Who is this dude in the red hat saying make America great again
America was made great because of people who looked like you
The same people who you now say their struggle was a choice
A choice to be raped, beaten, starved and murdered?
You have free thought and this is what you think
For a self-proclaimed genius you have no Common Sense
Behind closed doors of those you now embrace
You are a laughing stock and sadly misinformed
When they are done raping your legacy
You will come crawling back to the Black community
We are a forgiving and loving people
This time you've gone too far
It's okay to spread your wings
But a Black Man should never forget his roots or his people.

(Listening to *Never Let Me Down* by Kanye West)

Dean Jéan-Pierre

Moonwalking

Catchphrases become hashtags
Movements become selfie shots
Seems like we are a Generation Lost
Everyone proclaiming themselves a genius
When did genius need self-important accolades
Racism is now a new sport
One team seems to always lose
Being a Nigger now is somehow cool
Words once used to denigrate are now being fully embraced
It sometimes feels like the Twilight Zone
The world doesn't make sense anymore
Gun violence so rampant it feels like a videogame
Everyone wants a turn at having a kill
Fingers are always hot on the trigger
The cameras ready to feed social media
It's the only way we know how to communicate
As a Black Man my thoughts are all over the place
As I sit down to watch this play
I am the only Black face in an audience
Watching Black art applauded by white hands
You wonder, where are the rest of us to lend our support
Why aren't we here supporting the arts
This is how a culture gets lost
When it's too late we scream gentrification
When we were the ones not supporting our starving artists
Racism now wears a new face

RAGE

Recruitment starts from the White House
The country is doing the Moonwalk
Taking us right back to slavery days
It matters if you're Black or white, MJ had it all wrong
Something essential is being lost
Technology isn't our saving grace
I already think it's way too late
Even though we aren't yet in the last days
Something has to somehow change
Hate this deep remains a wound unhealed
Left untreated the stench is unbearable
We are at the tipping point on the edge of the world
Prayers and hopes won't save our souls
Even God seems to have washed his hands of us.

(Listening to *Keep Your Head* Up by Tupac)

If I Were a White Person

If I were a white person who understands how the world works
How rich folks really don't care about poor people,
Even those who are white
Unless there is a profit to be made exploited from their labor
I hope I would stand up for a cause
Stand up for a disenfranchised community who needed my voice
Use my white privilege to make a difference in this world
I hope I would be able to stand back, knowing I am privileged
Or least through no fault of my own
Living in a society that preaches equality
Yet still so divided by the concept of race
If I were a white person I would make no excuses
I would own the atrocities and crimes of my ancestors
Understanding my elevated status was earned through slave labor
Now it's my time to pay back unpaid wages
And call it social reparation
If I were a white person, I would ask myself
Why are dogs treated more humanely than Black people
And I know you say that's a hyperbole
But it sure doesn't feel that way to me
If I were a white person, I would ask myself
Why do I need to feel superior to other races
Why do I get so angry when they don't fall in line
Why do I still have that slave master mentality
Even as I preach the Bible and Christianity
If I were a white person

RAGE

I would hope the events of the world would trouble my soul
Even if I couldn't fully understand
The plight of the Black community
The first place to always start understanding is with empathy
And knowing the history of this country
There are still deep wounds which cannot be healed
Until the bandage is ripped off with an honest conversation
And, after that is said and done, we still need reparations
Reparations doesn't have to be monetary payment
It has to be something that can make a sustained difference
And with each passing generation,
Maybe then the legacy of slavery
Will become a footnote in history
A stain that can never, ever be fully erased
To ever forget would be to disgrace the memories of our ancestors
A history embraced will always be remembered
If I were a white person, I would examine my conscience
Place myself in the skin of a Black person and just be thankful
My daughters and sons
Never had to endure such inhumane treatment
Of having their minds, bodies and spirits systematically destroyed
Having their place in society constantly questioned
Imagine if your innocent children
Were ever treated as ours have been
Would you still want to pledge allegiance to a country
That sanctions such hate
Would you want to move on without a solution
If I were a white person in the land of the free

Dean Jéan-Pierre

And the home of the brave
These are the questions I would ask myself
If I am really searching for truth
If you're not,
Then wrap yourself in the flag and patriotism, go back to sleep
Leave it for the next generation who will do what you could not.

(Listening to *Freedom* by Beyoncé & Kendrick Lamar)

Modern Day Racism

Stay in your place
You are not welcome here
This is Somewhere, Anywhere in America
Even though you haven't broken the law
We don't feel safe with your kind around
These words aren't always said, but they are always felt
There is something about your Black body
Something I can't quite put my finger on
But it makes me fear for my life
So I will exercise my white right of privilege
Have you removed, just as a precaution
Then offer an insincere apology later on
This isn't the back of the bus
This isn't separate counters or water fountains
Or even the indignity of separate bathrooms
Modern day racism is filled with subtle pleasantries
Disarms you and makes you wonder
Maybe you are being too sensitive
After all, not everything can be about racism
It's that Jedi mind trick fucking with your perception
Stories of intolerance being captured all around the country
It's always us and not them being disrespected
It's always us being killed and arrested
Maybe next time you drive through my neighborhood
The cops will be called, just to see what happens
We are being shot with autonomy

Dean Jéan-Pierre

Lynched in the court system
Shot down in the streets like rabid animals
Jim Crow now wears his fancy suits
He no longer needs his white sheet to dress for work
He listens to our music filled with misogyny
He profits handsomely from our lyrical content
While devaluing our Black bodies and pacifying us with religion
Yet we claim we are being disrespected
When we won't respect ourselves
When we allow our women to fight our battles
We are the protectors of the home
Kings without a crown
A country we didn't want
But we are here now and must stand our ground
As we fight this resurgence of modern day racism.

(Listening to *The Revolution Will Not Be Televised*
by Gil Scott Heron)

Christians & Devils

Some wounds are just too deep to heal

Some sins you just cannot forgive

I am human and not a God

I just simply cannot turn the other cheek

But you know you must somehow forgive

Not for your oppressor's peace of mind but for yours

For the children you will raise

For the people you will love

For the community you are a part of

You cannot nurture the future and live in the past

The weight of hate will turn you into them

Some words cannot be reinvented and repurposed

Even when it is bastardized for commercial profit

The stench of blood lives in every syllable

A word birthed in hate cannot be reborn

So many Black people lynched, hanging like fruit

So many families ripped apart at the umbilical cord

Our women raped for pleasure and nine months later

Something beautiful is born for them to love

An innocent life born from hate

Our mothers and daughters,

Their bodies have been used and abused

For the pleasure of men on a first name basis with the Devil

Men who would then go home and pretend to be Christians

Reading Scriptures and quoting the Holy Bible to their children

Dean Jéan-Pierre

Time knows it doesn't have the answers
Even as it slowly tries to make us forget
We pray our children won't be judged by the color of their skin
Even though we know that they always will
We pray the Dream can still be attained
We pray for all these things on bended knees
To a God created in the image of our rapists and former Masters
If He looks like them, why would he choose to protect us
If He looks like us, why have we been made to suffer
I am angry by His neutrality as we die waiting for His mercy
Christians and Devils live in the shadows of good and evil
Black folks steadily praying to our blue-eyed, white savior
Hymns and prayers won't stop a bullet from spilling our blood
It's good to know most of us still somehow believe in God
Even when he is arbitrary with His love.

(Listening to *Choice of Colors* by The Impressions)

Wypipo (White People)

It's easy to blame wypipo for all our problems
They started the ball rolling with that slavery thing
They would like to conveniently forget that they are responsible
Erasing history is not as easy as an apology
Even though we haven't received one and never will
Not that it would make a difference in healing old wounds
It's easier to sweep these things under the rug
Let them become somebody else's problem
While urging the people wronged to just move on
Even as wypipo try to keep us in our place
We know the system is rigged against us
Every hill somehow gets steeper to climb
Every dream somehow gets harder to achieve
Every time we try to get ahead of the game
There's someone ready to change the rules and alter our future
The obstacles will always be there for us as Black people
It's just a fact of life for Black folks trying to get ahead
Post-racial is beautifully written fiction
I am always Black before I am African-American
One man gave us hope but couldn't save a country
The seeds of racism is woven deep into the fabric of this nation
It is as American as apple pie
To hate a Black man and don't know why
It is up to the collective individuals to do the work
To pass on the lessons learned from the past

Dean Jéan-Pierre

The job of repairing the Black family starts at home
The connective thread of personal responsibility
Will keep us rising until we reach the mountaintop
Even though some homes are broken, our spirit is not
Even though we are viewed as criminals, we are a proud people
Even though we can sometimes be our worst enemy
We can also be our greatest ally
Our women need us to be warriors for them, as they are for us
It is the only way the Black Family can mend
We don't always see the quiet reflection of greatness in ourselves
Wypipo cannot take that away from us,
Unless we give away our Black power
Every victory won is in repayment
For the past sacrifices of our ancestors
No matter your successes or failures, it does not end with you
There are others you can serve to inspire
This is how we win
When it becomes about Us and not Them.

(Listening to *Inner City Blues* by Marvin Gaye)

At Least I'm Not Black

I wonder what crosses your mind
When you see me about in the world
Especially in the climate we are living in today's society
Are you thankful that even though you don't have it all
Even though there are days when
You cannot monetize your white privilege
Maybe you can't take as many vacations as your parents once did
The American dream is getting harder and harder to fulfill
And maybe the world is scarier now than ever before
I am sure we share some of the same concerns for our families
My concern for my Black life living in this country
This is a reality that is not even on your radar screen
You hate to admit it but you know it's something you are thinking
At least I'm not Black and it's one less thing to worry about
You wouldn't change places with me
Even if I was rich and you were poor
It's not a conscious thought on your mind
As you make your way in the world
Maybe I would think the same thing if I were in your position
You come and go as you please
Never once having to worry about
Being a credit or discredit to your race
The world is your oyster and we are eating from different plates
Your place in the world is never questioned
Even in other countries you are viewed as being superior

Dean Jéan-Pierre

Not you as a person because, truth is, you are at best just ordinary
Not that there is anything wrong with that
You have been ascribed attributes
That you really haven't earned as an individual
The same way I have been but it's not to my benefit
You can leverage your whiteness
In a way my blackness would never allow
Every Black person knows this
But, for you, this is somehow a secret
Or at least you pretend not to be aware of the problem
My Blackness is a badge of honor for me
I know how many have died and suffered for this opportunity
I know how many backs have been broken so I can soar
I know how many dreams were never realized
Even though I am an individual
There is an added unspoken responsibility
I gladly accept for my people
It is the least I can do for everything I have been given
Being Black for me is not about labels of Blackness
Or about a color
It is about moving the culture forward for the next generation.
At least you're not Black, but I'm proud I am.

(Listening to *Sometimes I Feel Like a Motherless Child*
by Bessie Griffin)

Zoo Children

Brown children on display in cages like animals in a zoo
Their childhood exploited for political gain
The world watches as a tyrant is further emboldened
Free to run amok in a country known for checks and balances
Scriptures being perverted by politicians
And so called Christians in the name of God
When Muslims do it in the name of Allah they are called savages
When America does it, we are righteous and noble
The hypocrisy of a nation still haunted by the sins of slavery
A nation who rounded up its citizens
Like cattle in internment camps
Stole its ill-gotten land from the indigenous Americans
Now claim to be the moral authority of the world
Led by a man whose soul is bankrupt
Of any empathy for the innocent
God doesn't reside in the hearts of men like this
If such a God sanctions this morally abhorrent dogma
This is a God I cannot believe in, but I don't believe this is so
Children of God ripped from the arms of love
Placed behind bars
Like criminals being indoctrinated into a system
A new generation of anti-American sentiments
Is being groomed for destruction
This is where it begins
When people who have nothing are treated like animals

Dean Jéan-Pierre

Maybe not on this day, but the day is fast approaching
There will be a reckoning of sorts for this corrupt government
Fed by nativism and intolerance for other cultures
This is not how you make America great again
(Not that it ever was)
The melting pot wants to be one color
Purging all others in the name of God
Hope still spreads across this land,
Catching fire that cannot be extinguished
When good people of all races and creeds
Unite their voices in protest
When history demands your call to action
The bully, as all bullies do,
Will eventually fall to the will of the people.

(Listening to *Save The Children* by Marvin Gaye)

Never Broken

My spirit is never broken, even when I am bowed
The spilled blood of my ancestors runs upstream through my soul
Reminding me daily there is work yet to be done
Even though I may stumble, staying down is not an option
Much is expected of me because I demand it of myself
I am never broken because I am a soldier on the field of life
I am a role model for the others to follow
There were strong women in my life who showed me the way
There were men who weren't my father who gave me direction
Their example is my duty to share with the younger generation
Even when I am at my weakest
Even when I seem beaten, I am at my most dangerous
I will not bend; I will not break
When my story is told, when I am dead and gone
I want it to be one of inspiration
A beacon of light for those who have been forgotten, cast aside
I want my life to matter because in the times we now live
Hope is a commodity without investments
Dreams are too easily deferred because we fear hard work
I am never broken, never bowed
There isn't anything I cannot accomplish if I dare to dream
If I dare to step out of my box
And embrace life and all its possibilities.

(Listening to *We the People Who Are Darker Than Blue*
by Curtis Mayfield)

Dean Jéan-Pierre

BlackMan Nod

You don't know me
I don't know you
But we know the struggles of being Black in America
We know what it feels like to constantly look over our shoulders
The appearance of guilt, even when you are innocent
The belief you are an Other and not an American citizen
It is an American reality
Every Black Person understands implicitly
So we acknowledge each other as Black Men, as human beings
On the streets of America with a nod of the head
A silent but powerful affirmation of our shared history
It is an unpracticed ritual, but just as sacred
In this moment we are not invisible, we are seen
At any moment, everything can suddenly change
Encompassed in a BlackMan Nod is an entire conversation
It is a desire to let each other know you are not alone
It is an old school dap from another generation
The way we used to say good morning to our elders
It is a symbol of respect as we march through our day
A day at the office of climbing the slippery corporate ladder
Another day of having to prove yourself,
Even though you are just as credentialed
You have a Masters but the Massas don't care
They still see you as a nigger just dressed better
Maybe it's time you build your own
Maybe it's time we support each other

RAGE

Maybe we have said this before and nothing ever changes
Generational wealth cannot be acquired with a paycheck
Step out the box and create your own path
You don't know me, I don't know you
I see the stars, the moon and the sun shining in your eyes
It gives me hope that the dream is not yet deferred
Together we can create a brighter future
Together we can honor the sacrifices of our ancestors.

(Listening to *Someday We'll All Be Free* by Donny Hathaway)

Dean Jéan-Pierre

Black Girl Magic

We walk through this life knowing all eyes are on us
Waiting for us to fail and claim some sort of moral victory
Watching us with a curiosity not born of innocence
But a desire to own us, possess what is not for sale, anymore
Our bodies are talked and whispered about behind our backs
Our intellect questioned and not valued as equal
Our hair poked and prodded
As if on display for society's amusement
Our men are not always the first to defend us
Yet, we still love them fiercely
Because it is who we are as Black Women
Even after all these slights to dim our light
We find a way to rise to give life to our Black Girl Magic
It is a magic passed on from generations of Black Women
Women enslaved but never bowed
Chained but never broken
Beaten, raped, defiled and left for dead among the living
Their light was hidden but never stolen
Their hopes and dreams they passed down to their children
Endowing us with a strength we can call on when needed
I see my sisters in all walks of life, making their way in this world
Some have already walked into their purpose
Others are on the edge of discovering their true beauty
A beauty that emanates from deep roots bled into our souls
Beating fervently in our hearts a
And coming to life through the physical

RAGE

But manifesting its light into something spiritually beautiful
A magic you can touch and feel, even as it remains free to change
And evolve of its own choosing
The physical embodiment of our Black Girl Magic
Doesn't merely stop at what society objectifies
Our beauty is subtle, soft, nuanced, in your face, hidden
It is always evolving into something we have already imagined
But it is always there, waiting to be discovered,
Appreciated as something uniquely special
Not to be compared against any other women
Who are beautiful in their own right
Black Girl Magic was forged from a painful past
Left for dead, buried and reborn
Once held back by chains and closed minds
Never again.
Never again.
We are more than breasts, hips, thighs
And other dissected sexual parts
We are mind, body and spirit deserving of love
We are all links in a chain forged from a common legacy
A legacy that demands we claim what is rightfully ours,
Nothing more, and nothing less
We are here; we will be seen.
We are no longer invisible.

(Listening to *Black Pearl* by Sonny Charles & The Checkmates)

Dean Jéan-Pierre

Black Excellence

It doesn't matter how they view your life
It only matters how you see yourself
It is not for them to give you acceptance
It is not for them to allow you passage in this world
If you can only find your worth through their eyes
You will always be disappointed by what they see
Your reflection viewed through a prism of being a minority
You will always be viewed with a degree of curiosity
Black Excellence starts with us and not them
We are not defined by the acceptance of others
Before you judge me as inferior
Question the path of your supposed superiority
You afforded yourself every opportunity to prosper
While enslaving an entire generation with bigotry and brutality
Your four hundred-year head start wasn't earned with ingenuity
But with whips, chains and Scriptures you perverted
Your place in this world
Came at a price through oppressed people
The crown you wear was stolen from Kings and Queens
Mine was already paid for by my ancestors' free labor
The land you stole or conveniently discovered
Gentrification renamed as revitalization
You try to rewrite history while reliving it simultaneously
Homage to your oppression of us memorialized with statues
A daily reminder we cannot escape or forget
You lecture me on the morality of my race

RAGE

How we are prone to criminality

That we have too many babies

Our men are too lazy

Our women too loud

We are not your children in search of guidance

Never once have you taken responsibility

Or even an attempt at an apology

For all your crimes against my Black body

You have profited from my spilled blood

Made millions on the backs of my ancestors

While my people languish in the arms of poverty

You have waged wars against nations in the name of Christianity

The God you serve is foreign to me

Because the God you pray to at nights

Cannot condone such hatred

He cannot love and protect your family

Then condemn mine to hatred and bigotry

I reject such a God and will stand on my own

Black Excellence is a sustained movement, a relay race

The baton has been passed

With bloodied hands from our ancestors to us

Dropping it is not an option

Too many have died in anonymity

Too many have died wondering why God has forsaken them

Too many dreams have been deferred

Too many have worn the label of slave

Without being a human being first

For all those who will never feel the sweet breath of freedom

Dean Jéan-Pierre

To feel safe in their own person
You must stand tall and run the race for them
And when you are finally out of breath and given your last lesson
Pass the baton to the next person
There is a shift of consciousness afoot
Our children are waking up from their slumber
Putting away their video games and their sense of entitlement
They are a generation much maligned
They have been listening quietly
They are now ready to add their voice
They now have their marching orders
Many have died to secure your future
The world is watching
Will you answer the call beyond Black Lives Matter
Will you put the cause for justice before your own comfort
Will your anguish and anger become productive action
You are the sons and daughters of Martin, Malcolm and Rosa
She did not sit so you could relax
They did not die so you can call each other nigger
You are expected to rise beyond the ceiling
It is ready to shatter, so you just have to keep trying
The dreams of our ancestors are waiting to be fulfilled
Black Excellence was once denied by chains and bigotry
Mental slavery still exists in today's society
The lost sheep cannot be saved
Bigotry is on the upswing once again
Staying on the sidelines is not an option
You are called upon to act, to do your part
Will you listen to the whispers of our ancestors

RAGE

Urging you to not back down, to stand your ground
The warrior voice beating fervently in your soul
Demands you heed the call to activism
Bullets, hateful words and unjust laws are a stepping stone
On your way to Black Excellence
Arm your mind as a potential weapon
Get ready to do battle for your people
Use your thoughts as bullets to challenge the status quo
Fight the power in their arena with education
Take the village along with you on your journey
Black Excellence is not a dream, a figment of our imagination
It is as real as our first Black President.

(Listening to *Fight the Power* by Public Enemy)

Epilogue

Exhale now. Steady your hands. Calm your spirit. Have some tea, coffee, wine, maybe something stronger, meditate or pray. With the prose in RAGE, you have taken a walk in my mind, through the dark and the light. These are my daily thoughts you won't always see articulated on social media. I hope you felt the same range of emotions I feel: anger, despair, resiliency, sadness, tiredness, strength, and most of all, hope. When you are finished being angry, there has to be something there to sustain you, to inspire you to move forward. Anger does not sustain, hope does. Hope is what wakes us up in the morning to take another step in the fight for equality. A fight that didn't begin with us, but we are obligated to continue until we achieve the desired results. It has never been easy, but our ancestors stood at the forefront, knowing to fight back meant almost certain death. And still they stood their ground, not for themselves because the Promised Land was only in their imagination. They knew they would never stand on the mountaintop and bask in the glow of accomplishing their dreams. So they began the work and bestowed on us all their dreams, generation next.

Dean Jéan-Pierre

Rage is the fuel, the spark which gets us to participate in our destiny, our own story. When you participate, you control the narrative. No one is coming to save us. We must save ourselves. It begins with accountability. Hold the mirror to yourself first. Ask what more can you do, no matter how big or small. Every pebble in a pond is just as important to fill it as the first one. We are at a point in history when it feels like the forces of hate and intolerance are trying to turn the clock back, to make America great again. It has never been great for Black folks, just a steady walk towards getting better with each generation. Progress has been made but not enough. You are called upon to educate yourself, to think, to read, to travel, to engage in debate, to activism and community service. You are called upon to defend our women, to hold our men accountable when they fall short and to become engaged in the welfare of our communities. The days are short and we are called upon to wear many hats, to navigate many obstacles. And I know you are tired of constantly having to fight the same battles we thought had already been won. What choice do we have? The fight must go on. You must call upon strength you didn't know you had, but it's there. It vibrates in your bones and flows through your blood, waiting to be activated. I have seen its determination in the faces of our men and women. We come from a people who have had every conceivable obstacle placed in their path to deter their ascension, and still we rise, still we rise. The sun is getting warmer. Winter does not last forever. Spring is over the horizon, beckoning us to keep coming. We keep walking over hills, valleys and mountains without seemingly any end in sight. We have persevered through insurmountable odds and we continue to ascend. The journey has been long and along the way, we have struggled, sometimes despaired, but we have never given up. In this moment, in this generation, we will not be the generation that dropped the baton. Full steam ahead.

My Rage is filled with love for my people. It is always in service of wanting better for us. There are countless stories of our ingenuity, kindness, humanity that have remained untold. They need to be told to combat all the negative stereotypes of us. We are not a monolithic people and not the snippets of us captured on the evening news which then goes viral and somehow becomes truth. A history that remains silent cannot flourish and claim its rightful place for its people to shine. We are a proud people. We walk in confidence and expect to succeed, no matter the obstacles. The seeds have been planted. Water has sometimes been lacking. The shade allowed us to rest but we need to keep on moving. The sky is about to open. The deluge is on the way. Be ready. The floodgates of talent, opportunity and the moment are about to meet in this time in history. Claim your path. You are deserving of everything life has to offer. Use your Rage for something constructive. Don't let the daily assaults on our humanity, our right to be here as a people, make you question your place in this world. As Maya

Angelou eloquently said, "Your crown has been bought and paid for. Put it on your head and wear it." The spirits of those who suffered and died for our right to live in this world lives in those crowns. They are watching us like proud parents. Do their memories justice. You owe it to them, yourself, and the next generation.

6.20.18.

Just finished my second cup of coffee for the morning. I want to do something for someone today, whatever small gesture it might be. It is how we become a better society. It is how we begin to lift this cloud, making its way across this country. I hope RAGE sparked something in you. Inspired you in some way. I know you want more—there is no more. Well, who knows? Jéan-Pierre out!

The Black Guy

(Novel Excerpt)

1

IT'S NEVER SOMETHING that is ever said or even acknowledged, but you feel the weight of its presence wherever you go, your dark passenger, America's greatest imagined nightmare. It's a constant silent shadow, a reminder that even in the brilliance of sunlight, leaves you marked with a bullseye chalked around your body. You can almost feel the thoughts of your fellow human being standing in the elevator next to you. You almost want to sometimes tell them that you're okay—that you're one of the *good ones* and no harm will befall them, as you exist in their space, for a few seconds. You know how to be good around them and they will get back home safely to their family. *There is no need to panic.* You *almost* want to apologize to them for making them feel uncomfortable, but an apology by definition means you are doing something wrong. It means your existence has to be explained, as if Earth is not your home to and you somehow have less of a reason for being there than them. An apology makes you almost as culpable as them for their ignorance. You are not an immigrant on Earth, even when it feels as if we are living on two different planets. If you think about it too much longer, anger will well up inside of you, and spew hot like lava and you will morph into the angry black man they expect you to be. Luckily, the elevator door will chime in 5...4...3...2...1. *Freedom. Let freedom ring!*

A ride that takes five seconds feels like an eternity.

The white people in the elevator stare off into space, as if there is something that only they can see. You find yourself staring at the exact spot that they are looking at, because maybe, they are seeing something that your naked eye is missing. Maybe they have some sort of special eyesight that you are not privy to.

So you squint. *Nothing.*

You open your eyes wider. *Nothing.*

It occurs to you that they must have a lot on their mind: work, family, the state of the economy and wondering when black folks are finally going to take over because the President is black. You cough for no reason, except to make the silence less uncomfortable. Then it dawns on you, that maybe the President has it right. You can somehow turn all these feelings of being uncomfortable into a "teachable moment." So you turn to this other human being and with your best non-threatening smile (not sure what a threatening smile looks like), which you hope doesn't make you look too constipated, you say something innocuous like, *feels like snow is coming,* how about those (fill in appropriate sports team) or *I am not going to hurt you.* Saying "I'm not going to hurt you" is almost as bad as when white folks say,   "I'm not a racist, but..." You hope your smile lets them know that you come in peace, as the Indians were once told, but as you turn to open the door to a brief conversation, you notice the recoil, that sudden burst of fear in their eyes, as if they are the ones in danger. History has proven this to be false. It's too late for you to shut the door. You are caught between a half-assed smile and the need to scream, *what the fuck is wrong with you.* If you do that, then the label of the angry black man becomes your epitaph. You should have just minded your own damn business, ignore them also by staring at invisible alien creatures in the ceiling, wait for the door to chime open and return their fake smile as you exchange words of have a good day.

If they could somehow get that Harry Potter invisibility cloak or teleport their ass out of here, say into a less dangerous situation, like a holdup or a fight, then they would. Their reaction angers you, even when you expect it. You feel your smile turning into a sneer. You want to use your hand like a windshield wiper and clear your face of your impending anger, but it's too late. Anger alert! Your sneer greets their fear and it's a standoff of the races in an elevator death cage match. They are praying for the fucking elevator door to open to release them from this prison, so they can run out as if reenacting a scene from *Psycho.* The sadistic side of you somehow hopes that the elevator malfunctions and just the two of you will be trapped in it for a few hours. But you know you won't be able to maintain the "sneer of black anger" that society has come to expect. You will in 5…4…3…2…1 revert to your momma's baby boy and flash that winning smile that makes women drop their draws, old black women pinch your cheeks and old black men slap you on the back, because they see themselves in you.

Have a nice day, the other human being says to you as the elevator door releases them into the world. Their smile is Botox tight. They will probably need a drink, even though it's only eight in the morning. You can almost hear them recounting to their other human friends later on about their harrowing elevator ordeal. The details will be embellished. You will be a story at a dinner party as their friends commend them for their bravery. One of them might even blog about the experience and by the time you log on to Facebook or Twitter, you will be trending ahead of the situation in Syria, the economy or some innocent person getting killed because they fit a profile of fear. By the time they are finished, you will have suddenly morphed into a seven-foot version of Shaquille O'Neal, complete with a Fu Manchu and dangling earrings the size of horseshoes. In fact, let the record show that you are only a measly five-ten, barely lean (whatever that means) and almost anyone could kick your black ass (more so brownish like an oatmeal cookie) if they have a gym membership. But none of that matters. The color of your skin introduces who you are. It says hello for you. It lets white folks assume/believe/know/suspect that there is a potential for danger, even though you have never spent a day of your life in jail (you are not the exception to a life free from a jailhouse holiday). The closest you have ever been to a jail is when you sent your brother a few nudie magazines through the mail and of course, the obligatory COPS show where there is always a black shirtless male running from the law. Your brother made sure to tell you that the staples have to come out or else they will be confiscated. His girlie magazines were his Bible. He prayed to random tits and ass with a reverence that would make any man sweat. You try not to imagine your brother jerking off in jail, just so he can remain calm, release his stress and do his bid. So far, that's been your only experience with an inmate. It's already assumed that "more than likely" you've done time, and if you haven't — then at some point in your life, you will be behind bars, and then they can say, see I told you so, it was only a matter of time. And as they continue to spin this tale of epic Steven Spielberg/Quentin Tarantino proportion, their friends who have gathered are filing away this *experience.* Next time they enter an elevator, that experience will somehow become their reality, without so much as a word being exchanged when they encounter a black male. Miscommunications without a word being said, now that either takes a lot of talent, or the allowance of fear and preconceptions change your perception of what you are seeing.

There are times when I feel as if I am being viewed in the third person and hardly ever as the first person, where I can be more authoritative. I want to be Langston Miller and not *the black guy*. I want to know when I enter a room that I can blend in, without my color putting a bullseye on me. Everything I do and say will be viewed through the narrow prism of race. Without even wanting to, I am the spokesman for my race. If I pass the invisible test of acceptance, then the next black person will have it easier, but if I fuck up, then your black ass is fucked. Without knowing me the next black person will think, someone fucked up before and now I have to pay for his shit—ain't that a bitch. I would like all of that to be untrue and believe it's just some black fairytale, but I know it's all served in truth because being judged immediately for the color of your skin is here to stay, just like reality shows. Profiling is as American as apple pie and Columbusing. I still don't understand how reality shows have made it so far, but that's an argument for another day. You would think that at some point the public would wake up and say heh, like Willie Mays, I've been fooled long enough. No more bamboozling me with television fake drama that should be taking place in someone's living room—where are the real stars and television shows. But *nooooo*—people love this shit. By people I mean black and white people. There is no separation of taste and class anymore. It's all become muddled water that folks pretend to turn their noses up at, but you know they are watching when they get home. It's a guilty pleasure we don't want to admit. It's like men who love prostitutes, but few of us will ever admit to it. Lots of men love prostitutes because they knows instinctively what's on your perverted mind. You don't have to articulate what you want her to do—she just does that shit—because she's a prostitute— it's her job. It's one of those things that women should just assume about men without even bothering to ask them. "Honey, do you like prostitutes?" What's the poor bastard supposed to say to a question like that? There is only answer you can give. Don't bother trying to explain your reasons for loving prostitutes. Just answer with a resounding no. She will know you are lying. You know you are lying. But it's one of those lies that come with a wink and a nod. It keeps the peace because there will always be something else to argue about later. Never admit to liking prostitutes because your woman will then have proof that you're a pervert. It becomes harder for her to lie to her friends that you're a good man. You can still be a good man and love prostitutes, but women have a prism of their own.

The elevator door slides open and before I can even step out, a middle-aged white man tries to get on. I guess the elevator will leave him behind or something. I stand my ground, even without the law on my side because sometimes you must. He stares icily at me. I do the same. I almost want to cue the iconic Clint Eastwood western theme song. Finally he steps aside and I get off. It's not a victory or anything that requires an NFL dance in the end zone after a touchdown. It might give him pause the next time an elevator door opens. It's just common courtesy. Everyone is always in a fucking rush to get where? They are in a rush to get to work, but then bitch all day about their jobs on social media.

2

PEOPLE WHO WORK in the building rush by me on the street, no one looks up. Their heads are buried in their phones. They are intent on getting to work and the winter cold sweeps into the building with them, bringing all the negative and positive energy in their lives into this one confined space. They are either late or have to use the bathroom after enjoying their first cup of coffee.

It's hard to tell sometimes how folks are feeling because their faces never tell you who they are. The public masks we wear to fend off invisible intruders into our personal space becomes part of your persona. Sometimes you forget which face you are wearing. I have done it myself. Sometimes on the Blue line train morning commute into Washington, DC from Maryland, I put on my headset, even though the music is turned off. I want the world to leave me alone as I get myself mentally ready to take on the day. No talking. I don't want to make small talk. What is small talk, except being kind when you really just want to be left alone in your own world. Small talk makes others feel better about themselves, something they can tell their friends later at a dinner party, and again you become an anonymous storyline to make someone else seem more interesting or some sort of benevolent human being. They can brag about reaching out to someone they would never normally have spoken to and they gleamed some much needed insight into the way another race or culture survives. "It's quite remarkable," you can imagine them commenting as they sip on a glass of wine, all pretentious and shit. In a five minute chat on a noisy commuter train, they have become an expert on race relations and can now go into the world, toss out random talking points about a group of people, they have only seen on television and snippets of news clips. All it took to gather these deep, probing insights was making small talk standing face to face on a packed subway, waiting in line at the post office or in Starbucks and sitting next to someone at the movies before the obligatory commercial asking you to turn off your cell phone, so that everyone can enjoy the movie.

A brisk wind wraps around my face and sticks to it like a piece of wet plastic. Even though Starbucks is only a quick two minute walk away, I button up my Peacoat and shove my hands deep into its pockets. My fingers curl around some loose change and what feels like a cold piece of French fry which I toss into an overflowing garbage. The cold gets inside of your clothing, sticks to your skin like a needy lover and refuses to let you go. It can be quite discomforting to feel cold, even when you are surrounded by heat. Maybe it's why people drink so much coffee or like smokers, they just need to have something in their hand. It makes them feel useful. When a coffee drinker gets down to that last sip, a panic attack ensues because taking the last sip leaves them with an empty cup on their walk to work. So instead of drinking it, they wet their lips with it, until they arrive at work and make a mad dash to the cafeteria for a refill.

The line is already out the door. It's a new Starbucks on 20th and L. The previous tenant was a small coffee shop of the mom and pop variety. I hope they stuck up Starbucks like a robber in a bank and got as much money as they could. These days you don't pay for quality. You pay for the name. The name means more because it means that you are a better person if you frequent places that everyone knows. Folks see you walking down the street with a Starbucks cup, they make assumptions about you. It's another kind of profiling, but it's encouraged. I have co-workers who refuse to drink the no brand coffee that our company furnishes for free. It doesn't taste the same, they say. They need their Starbucks to feel alive, they say. It's all bullshit. It's just another way of letting complete strangers know something about you, without them having to ask. Today is Thursday, so it's payday. It's my bi-weekly Starbucks treat to myself.

It must be close to twenty degrees. My face feels frozen, but it retains its brown complexion. The faces of most of the people waiting in line are various shades of pink and light red. I almost feel sorry for them, but it's a choice to wait in line for something you can get at work for free. A homeless black man shuffles up and down the line asking for spare change. Everyone shakes their head without looking at him. Most of them ignore him completely and continue to check their phones and update their social media statuses which is more important than a man begging for a cup of coffee.

"All you motherfuckers have no money to help out the homeless, eh?" He screams in frustration. "But you can afford a five dollar cup of fucking coffee, go back to your warm office and act like you don't see me. Coldhearted motherfuckers!"

A brave voice shouts from the line. "How do we know you're not going to buy liquor or drugs?" The silence of the crowd is an implicit agreement. They were all thinking the same thing, but had the common sense, decency or cowardice to keep their opinions to themselves. There is always one fool ready to step out on the ledge and take one for the team, even though no one asked him to.

The homeless man turns to face the crowd searching for the voice. The stench of his unwashed body catches a ride on a cold wind and makes it way slowly through the crowd. I swallow his rancid scent, but my facial expression remains stoic. A few people cough and murmur obscenities under their cold breath. They know better than to antagonize him. He doesn't have much more to lose. The last thing you want to happen early in the morning is to get shot. Well, no   one wants to get shot at any time during the day.

"If I had any money, I would bet most of you righteous motherfuckers had a few drinks last night and the other half dabbled in some weed or cocaine." No one said a word. Silence of the guilty. "If there's anyone who needs a fucking drink it's the homeless because we have to put up with all this self-righteous bullshit." He motions with both hands and points a finger at the crowd. "Don't fucking judge me. You don't know my goddamn life and half the shit I've been through."

His insanity must be fueling his body temperature and keeping him warm. He isn't wearing a coat, just a dirty blue sweater with layers of other sweaters and shirts. His fingers are exposed through his gloves. The tips are cutoff like a biker. A wool hat which looks like a bowl of Fruit Loops with all the colors covers his head. I am right by the door. Every time it opens various flavors of the crowd's coffee addiction teases my nostrils. You can almost hear the people in line outside the store inhaling, gulping and fiendish for a taste, just before it closes again.

He is standing next to me now, staring straight ahead. I wonder if he might attack me, but I quickly dispel that notion, even though it's possible. I slow my breathing down to avoid inhaling his pungent scent. I am one step away from freedom and from his judgment.

"I expected more of you, brother," he says quietly. So quietly it is barely above a whisper. He sounds like a disappointed parent scolding a child. I hate when strangers call me brother. I understand the implied comradery, but it leaves me wanting to ask them questions. It is a shared brief moment which should require no explanation other than that we share similar struggles. "These white folks see me out here hustling and wonder why I can't get a job. They don't know me or owe me anything, even though it would be quite human of them to assist another human being down on his luck. But you, my brother, you look like you read, and even if you don't—you should always help a fellow black man out."

My anger boils and I turn to face him. His eyes are sad. Sadder than I would have thought. I hold on to my indignant anger. "How do you know I just didn't help another homeless person down the block?"

"Did you?"

His question is calm and logical. I didn't expect it. I don't answer him.

"People give because they want to and not because you bully them."

"Sometimes it's the only way they will give. Guilt is a very useful tool when folks who are more privileged seem unable to empathize." His eyes never blinks as he stares me down. He was daring me to say something to defend something that was indefensible. It's like defending a fucking rapist or pedophile.

"What would you like to drink?" I finally asked him. I felt like a waiter.

"Trenta Caramel Macchiato with some extra caramel sauce, please."

The look on my face cannot hide my thoughts. I suppose it's what white people feel like when they have been caught having a thought that shows their ignorance. All of us don't read urban books or erotica. Some of us enjoy Malcolm Gladwell, Wally Lamb, Kurt Vonnegut, Alice Hoffman and countless other white writers.

"Not because I'm homeless doesn't mean I don't have good taste and know what a fucking Trenta is."

He bitch slapped me without raising a finger.

I quickly ordered my drinks and the smiling young blonde girl took my name. It's too early for such a bright smile. That's a nice touch by Starbucks, to personalize your order. I feel as if I am walking into *Cheers* and everyone knows my name. *Langston!* All the baristas scream and I would wave and take a bow. They already know my order because they know my name. It makes people feel important, special. It makes people feel less invisible. They might go the entire rest of the day without ever having someone call their name and be happy to see them. It's a small thing, but then again it's not. Checkmate, Starbucks.

Customers thirsty for a taste of their drinks fidget with their phones. They look lost and in need of a caffeine drug hit. Hoping that the next name called will be theirs. When someone's name was finally called their face brighten and they snatch their prize from the barista, quickly putting their liquid gold treasure to their nose, then their lips and swallowing gluttonously. It was like being picked for their high school team and not being last. Stigma stings. It grows up with you.

"Langston!"

My instinct is to smile; gloat, but I suppress it. I feel envious eyes on me. They want an explanation. Maybe it's my imagination. So this is what being privileged feels like. It's a small dose, but I will take it.

"I was here before him," I hear a whiney male voice exclaim when I turn my back to walk away. "I'm already late," the whiner continues, as if he is the only one on earth who has to get to work.

Shut the fuck up, bitch. The words are in my eyes, but they will never cross my lips. This is not how I behave in public. My public persona is always calm, rational, even when I have felt warranted anger. I don't need to see his face to know who he is. It is the face of entitlement having to wait in the back of the line. It feels as if I have won something, even though my prize is yet to be determined.

The line has dwindled as I exit the store. My eyes quickly scan the area for the homeless guy. I finally see him about half a block away pushing his shopping cart. One of the wheels is bent and his cart keeps falling over, scattering all his worldly position. I quicken my pace to catch up with him.

"Here's your coffee. Sorry about being an asshole earlier."

He stares at me with a vacant look as we wait for the stoplight to change. He takes the coffee without saying a word and walks away. My good deed for the day goes unrewarded without even so much as a thank you. This would be a good status for my Facebook page, I think to myself. But then I think, what kind of asshole goes on Facebook to rant about giving a homeless guy a cup of coffee and gets pissed off because he wasn't thanked properly. Only a schmuck does something like that. Am I a schmuck? Schmucks don't buy homeless people coffee that costs five bucks. A schmuck would tell him to go to a homeless shelter where it's warm and the generic coffee is free.

I watch him for a minute as he slowly disappears down the block, past Dominoes and then Subways. A few pedestrians rush by me, but I stand my ground. I was here first. For a brief moment I consider following him, just to see how he lives but decide against it. Seeing it won't change anything for either of us. He stops at the corner, lifts the cover from his Trenta cup of coffee, smells it, and tosses it in the garbage. I just wasted fifteen minutes pay on this guy. Fucking homeless people, they don't know the value of a dollar and hard work. That's the last time I help out someone who needs help.

3

THE ELEVATOR IS packed when I step inside. No one moves to make space, so I say excuse me and fit myself into the herd of people. Luckily someone has already pressed my floor. I am always fearful of drinking coffee in a packed elevator. What if the elevator suddenly stops and my cup goes flying and burns someone? A good cup of coffee gone to waste. I can wait twenty seconds to get to the tenth floor before drinking it. It's not life or death.

The door slides close, but someone waves their hand between the closing doors and it reopens. Just to get on an elevator, you risk losing your hand? The things we do so we won't have to wait, what, another thirty seconds for another elevator to come down. Music is blaring from his headphone when he enters. The packed elevator feels like a nightclub, as if we should all break out into a dance, but this crowd doesn't seem like the dancing type. They are more interested in their smartphones and what's trending on social media. No one says a word, but everyone is thinking the same thing—they must be. He sings the misogynistic lyrics out loud as if he is alone in the elevator—as if he is in a soundproof   recording studio. Every other word is *bitch*, followed by obligatory *nigger*. Everyone else on the elevator is white, except us. I want to ask him to turn it down. No one needs to hear our private business or how we address each other. Every word he utters, it is with a relish of defiance, as if daring anyone to ask him to be quiet. Of course, no one will. We stand side by side. I am dressed for corporate America. He dresses to piss off corporate America. I would be invited into a home in polite society, while he would have to wait outside. Standing next to him at this moment, there is no difference. We are viewed the same. If something goes down, I will be guilty by association of color. I know this. He doesn't seem to give a shit.

The beat is catchy. It's Dr. Dre featuring Snoop Dogg. The music sounds clearer. It's coming through those Beats headphone by the good doctor. From NWA (Niggers With Attitude) to Apple. It's the ultimate fuck you to America by a rap artist. The elevator pops open on five. It's a mass exodus. I can only imagine the conversation which will ensue.

"Can you believe that shit?" One middle-aged white man will say.

"It's okay for them to call themselves niggers, but let a white person say it and all of a sudden they want to go all Sharpton and Black Lives Matter on your ass," a young white male versed in hip-hop culture will retort.

"It's so unfair. If you don't say it with malice, then I don't really see the problem," a naïve young woman might chime in as she sips on her Chai Latte.

"The fact that you don't see the problem worries me," an elderly grandmotherly type responds. "You know how it feels when someone tells you that you have to do something, regardless of their intent—you automatically bristle and want to smack the shit out of them. It's the same thing with that word. It makes every black person want to slap every white person who thinks they can say that word and not get a visceral response."

It's what I imagine their conversations would be, but usually with race, people have these conversations inside their heads and not with each other. Thoughts get jumbled in your head. Your fears begin to make sense to you, because the only rational voice you're hearing is yours, inciting you to explore your deepest reservations and prejudices. If you are able to get out of your own head, hear the words you're thinking out loud, while you voice them to another person, then your ignorance becomes a matter of record. When you hear your thoughts translated to words when speaking to someone, the absurdity of how you feel becomes obvious, sometimes anyway.

"See how those white folks couldn't wait to get off the elevator." He had turned off the music, removed the black headphones from his head and laughed out loud. I guess it was a joke that I was supposed to understand because we share the same color. Mine is brown like toast. His is dark like late evening. But in the world we are black. "Shit never gets old every time I do it."

"So you've done this before?"

"All the time, dude. Shit is hilarious to see some white folks reactions. I should record them and post that shit online on Twitter. That shit would get a million hits, son."

I want to tell him that I'm not his son. He looks a few years younger than me. First I will be his son, then later on in the conversation, I will graduate to being his nigger. None of those words appeal to me. Nigger felt dirty on my tongue, as if I was saying something that should be kept a secret and never revealed.

He grins and is waiting for my response. For me to high-five him, as if we are sticking it to whitey. It is sadder when we dehumanize each other and then get upset when another group of people do it. Dehumanization carries no lesser or greater weight because it is perpetuated by someone else or another group. It would hurt me more when someone who knows my struggles still chooses to disrespect me, instead of honoring our common path to claiming a right, which is our humanity, instead of being regarded as a privilege.

Not saying anything only empowers him to continue doing what he is doing. There is not enough time on this elevator ride to explain to him the error of his ways, the ugliness of his words. Arguments I am sure he is quite well aware of. He seems to be an intelligent person. His manner of dress shouldn't preclude him from the intelligence gene pool. Dressed in oversize jeans. Under his open black jacket, his blue shirt is also unbuttoned, revealing a t-shirt emblazoned with a Tupac Shakur photo. Tattoos adorn his neck like a rock star or basketball player. I am sure he has many more decorating his body. His entire persona is a statement of rebellion. There is not enough time to voice my opinion, so I give him a half-hearted smile. He assumes he has my approval. I cannot hear the music from his headphone anymore, but he is singing the hip-hop anthem, *Fight the Power.* His two hands are raised as if reaching for the sky and he screams *fuck the man,* which seems ironic these days, considering who the head Negro in charge is. The elevator door chimes open, closes behind of me and just like that, he is gone. It is as if he never existed in my life. Just like that.

4

THE SECURITY DOOR requires an access code to enter the suite to my job. A few times I have forgotten my key pass and had to wait for someone to get off the elevator or come out to get coffee to let me in. Usually no one questions me, they just allow me entry. I am aware that I look safe. With the appearance of looking safe comes some understood privileges which are never given voice. A white colleague opens the door, gives me the perfected smile and I reciprocate with my black perfected smile. He has saved me from the hassle of having to explain myself or calling my supervisor to leave his office to allow me entry.

The long corridor leading to my cubicle is empty. The walls are lined with pictures of smiling employees at their work stations. It's a simple message. *Book Me Now* is a good place to work. It is like most relationships, you tolerate it, until you can do better. We are one of the top five Indie publishing houses in the country, according to Publishers Weekly. Writer's Digest did a spread on a few of the agents/editors/customer service/publicists, of which I was one of them and because of that one story, everyone who   thinks they can write or has the next best-selling novel is submitting their novel to us, especially me. With the explosion of EBooks and self-publishing, the literary game has become like *American Idol*. Everyone thinks they can write, even if they have never taken a writing course, read E.B White's *Elements of Style*, studied the greats of their genre—or any genre, but all of the sudden, they wake up one morning and have the brilliant idea that they too can become the next Terri McMillian, Eric Jerome Dickey or Zane. Most of these new age social media *writers* forget that it's a craft. One doesn't learn a craft in a day and suddenly decide that they are Picasso or Shakespeare. I blame reality television for fooling untalented people into believing that somehow all common sense goes out the window, and just by the sheer will of wanting to win—that they deserve to win. The same attitude of entitlement has bled into the literary field. Where else but in this field can anyone just literally walk off the street, write a shitty book, stamp a label on it, *National Bestseller* and no one even knows who the fuck they are? I will tell you where, in this social media era meshed with reality television I want to be famous at all cost mentality. It's obscene, but else can you expect in a country where bad sex video gets you famous and twenty years of hard work gets you a pink slip. I will take leave of my high horse for a moment, climb down to my soapbox and suppress the urge to vent some more.

From the other end of the corridor walking towards me is

one of our publicists, Kevin. Short, stocky, hairline receding, but holding onto it tighter than a black woman with a bad weave. The hallway is long, narrow, so it's impossible not to see someone walking towards you. I keep to my right, he stays on his left, no one has to give way. I take a sip of my coffee and get ready to acknowledge him, to say good morning. My eyes find his face and search his eyes. His eyes are the color of the sky and searching the ceiling for invisible clouds. I don't bother looking, there is nothing there. I keep my good morning to myself and we cross paths like strangers. At least he didn't pull out his cell phone and do the fake phone call bit or look down to stare at the uninteresting carpet, again. Situations like this you want to say something, to make someone acknowledge you or least find out why saying good morning is so difficult. But then saying something then makes it a *thing*. They become uncomfortable and apologize profusely. It's nothing racial they will think, but cannot use those words. And you then feel obligated to smile and say something trite to defuse an awkward situation. Maybe you misunderstood the intent of walking right by you as if you didn't exist for the third time this week. Maybe saying good morning to a fellow co-worker is no big deal and you should be thankful for their silence, that way you don't have to strike up an asinine conversation about the weather, sports and whatever topical bullshit that is trending on social media. Maybe, in a way, they are doing you a *huge* favor by walking right you as if you were a black ghost.

I need to take a leak. Drinking coffee always sends me running to the bathroom. It disgusts me when I see men take their coffee mugs into the bathroom. They leave it on the urinal or take it into the stalls with him as they do their business. I place my Starbucks cup on top of a file cabinet in the corridor. It's a cabinet which contains thousands of unread manuscripts, not because they are unpublishable, but because we have not gotten to them as yet. Self-Publishing is an industry without any rules. If you can pay, we will publish you. It's a never-ending money tree because everyone has a dream, and there is always someone looking to exploit your lack of talent to achieve that dream.

The stench in the bathroom makes me gag. It's too damn early for someone to leave their home and come to work to drop a skunk bomb in the bathroom. This is why I don't bring my coffee cup into the bathroom. The stinking fumes will get into your coffee, mix its stench flavor into your drink, and you end up drinking some stranger's foul shit odor. It may sound far-fetched, but stranger things have happened. I push out my urine in an urgent stream as I tried to hold my breath, but I'm not a fish, so I have to exhale and inhale the rotten odor into my lungs.

The bathroom door swings open as I lather my hands in cheap soap. The immediate reaction of disgust makes me tense up and get ready to defend a crime that I did not commit. It is the CEO of the company, Nathan Bradford.

"Jesus Christ—what the fuck is that smell?" He yells in disgust before he sees me washing my hands at the sink. "Oh, sorry Langston," he mumbles when he sees me. "Didn't know you were still in here."

I wanted to say it wasn't me, but it would make an awkward situation even worse. Whoever it was that did this was walking around without having to take responsibility for this act. It's hard to make conversation with your boss in a smelly restroom, when he is thinking you're the culprit of some foul smelling animal odor.

"Had to take a leak. Coffee always does it to me."

"Yeah, me too," he answers absently as he walks down to the urinal.

The bathroom was quiet enough that I could hear his zipper coming down. I stood in front of the sink, but not too close. Water always pools around the edges, and with the khaki pants I was wearing, it would look like I pissed myself if I got wet. My Malcolm X glasses looks good on me, at least that's what my girlfriend, Shana, told me when she helped to pick it out a few weeks ago. It makes you look more militant and your boss will take you more seriously, she had said. I was hesitant because I preferred the scholarly look to the angry black man militant look. The latter doesn't get you too far in corporate America these days. Something as simple as a pair of glasses can stereotype you, or the way you wear your hair.

The glasses were more of a fashion statement than any anything having to do with a political statement or ideology. All the white guys in the office thought it was cool, so I kept wearing it.

The only sound in the bathroom was the running water in the sink, acting as a buffer between us. In meetings we were chatty, cordial, in our element of professional conversation. But here in the bathroom, small talk felt, well, *small.* I stared at my reflection in the mirror, and even though I knew it was me, the eyes staring back looked like a stranger. It wasn't the first time I had felt this odd sensation as if the person trapped inside the mirror was the real me trying to claw his way to the surface. I could see in his eyes that he wanted to have a conversation, to warn me of things that he somehow knew, but I would not believe. Every time I saw those eyes in a mirror, staring back at me, I would quickly avert his gaze, before I started thinking too much. Too many thoughts will lead you down an alley filled with dangerous questions, and by the time you exit the darkness in search of light, the light remains dim.

My boss and I are dressed like Ebony & Ivory twins.

Khaki pants. Blue Gap buttoned down shirt.

His glasses are stylishly rounded. Mine is a throwback to militancy. My fashion statement without having to put in any of the work.

Our eyes meet as we wash our hands. The joke is obvious,

but it remains unsaid.

Instead he utters, "nice glasses." It sounds like a compliment, but it could have been a subtle warning. I didn't want to think like my father and believe that white people said one thing, and meant another. My father has a healthy, paranoid distrust of the white man. It was up to you to figure out what they really meant and get to the kernel in the maze of their thoughts, he would always tell me. Maybe that's why he enjoyed playing chess so much. Paranoia makes you question everything.

"We will go over the third quarter numbers later," he says. He had walked away before I could formulate a response. I didn't want to pull a George Costanza of *Seinfeld* and come back with a response hours later. What I wanted to say was *the numbers are fine. We are on track to surpass last quarter's numbers.* I would remember it for the meeting at ten. It would be too late by then. The door swung close and he was gone.

The person in the mirror smiled back at me. It was the kind of smile someone gives you to instill confidence in yourself. I should not need that kind of reassurance. But every edge, false or imagined, gets you to your next goal. I was the only black male on staff, and even if there wasn't any indirect pressure by management or my colleagues, I felt a responsibility to prove myself every day. Not because I didn't think I didn't measure up, but when you're the odd one in a group, everyone is looking at you to fuck up. If you succeed, then that's beautiful, but if you fuck up, then it will be something that was already expected. I didn't want to be the exception. I wanted to prove to my co-workers, my father, and yes, myself, that I belonged and it had nothing to do with me being black. Race was something I was conscious of in subtle ways, but I had never had any direct encounters with racism. I might be the only black male in America never to have a negative encounter with the police. Was it just dumb luck? My father would say, my time hadn't come as yet to have a story to tell. I believed that I didn't call undue attention to myself. I minded my own business and just carried myself in a certain way, that didn't turn my innocence into being viewed as an automatic suspect. Innocent until proven guilty. I believed that and lived my life by those words.

5

MY CUBICLE IS my second home. I spend more time in it, than I do in my own one bedroom apartment. It's about the size of a tiny one bedroom apartment in Manhattan. It has its own door to slide open and close. It comes equipped with space to hang my coat and cabinets and drawers to store manuscripts, snacks and other junk that I keep meaning to bring home. My cubicle roommates haven't arrived as yet, so I still have a few moments of quiet before their incessant talking would drive me near the brink of madness. Anytime it got to be too much, I would walk away and take a mental break outside.

I flipped on my computer screen and waited for it to wake up. It slowly changes from black to blue. While I waited, I checked my voicemails. The first was from my Dad reminding me not to forget that we were meeting for dinner this evening at Busboys and Poets on 14th and V Street, promptly at eight. One of his favorite local poets would be on the mic tonight. He was a man who relished being on time to every event. The next ten messages were from writers who had unrealistic expectations of their books that were not being met. Most of them assumed that all they had to do was write a book—and the money would start rolling in—Oprah would call them and life would be a bowl of cherries. The landscape of the publishing industry in the last year is ever changing. Everyone thinks they are a writer these days. It seems that there is almost a writer for every person in the world. Everyone has a story to tell and EBooks has become the great equalizer in the literary world. It has given people who would not have a shot in hell of getting a publishing contract with one of the major publishing houses, a chance to be heard. With the birth of a new industry, there are generally soft rules, so sharks are lurking everywhere to prey on the dreams of the uninformed, even though the power of free information is just a Google click away. Every book I have helped to publish since I've been here, I believe in, but in self-publishing, there is almost no budget for marketing. Bombarding social media pages with book blurbs and pleas of *please buy my book* is not exactly marketing. It's more like new age literary stalking. I haven't had a breakout success yet at *Book Me Now.* The pressure is on me to find a book that will break through. It's the reason why I was lured to this company from my previous employer. I chose money over prestige. I was still living off my reputation of discovering a young Caribbean writer from St. Lucia and turning his book of his short stories about growing up on the island, *Sun Kisses My Skin,* into a modest hit. I tried using my success to leverage more money, but I was quickly rebuffed. Stung by my rejection, I fled to this up and coming publishing house. My father said I overplayed my hand   too quickly. I disagreed. Money doesn't make a man he counseled me. That was the extent of his advice. My father is old school. He doesn't understand today's business world. You have to strike while you're hot or else you are quickly forgotten, like yesterday's news.

I did my usual rounds of my Facebook pages. Humans of New York. Publishers Weekly. Treasure Blue and Kisha Green (they are always dropping jewels about the industry). Paulo Coelho. He always has insights that I appreciate and put into action. Novel Nerds and Word Porn. I enjoy their anecdotes on books. It's part of my job to search through social media, for something—anything. One day you could just get lucky and discover the next literary star posting excerpts of their unpublished book on Facebook and Instagram. It can happen. It happened with Justin Bieber and look at him now. Granted it's music and not literature, but the same mechanics are in place for success.

My inbox on Facebook was overflowing with requests from writers for me to read their manuscripts. Some were pretty civil. Other guaranteed that their book was the next *Fifty Shades of Grey*—as if that is a good thing. Then there were those, which were the majority, who had no business trying to write a book, but someone along the way boozed up their head with the idea that they could actually write. So now we have this phenomenon of everyone wanting to write a book, to become a bestselling writer. Being a writer is as common a dream as wanting to be a basketball player or a singer. The literary world should have someone like Simon Cowell to tell some folks that they have no business trying to write. Some of the "manuscripts" I've read were just painful reading. Adults should be ashamed that they went to school and still cannot write a decent sentence or know the difference between your and you're. Their and there. It's and its. The list goes on and on. From this quicksand of literary gems, I am supposed to find the next Ta-Nehisi Coates, Walter Mosley or K'wan. All of my colleagues are doing what I am doing right now, just on different pages. No one is thinking out the box on how to find fresh new talent. I ponder this for a few minutes as I click aimlessly from page to page. Stories of the latest celebrity scandals pop up everywhere. Fight videos are now popular but I never watch those. Women posting pictures with their asses hanging out and wondering why men are not asking them about what's on their mind. Social media is just reality television gone amuck. Only difference is that you're exposing your life for free, while the attention whores on television are getting paid. Everyone wants their fifteen minutes of fame these days and they don't care how they get it. Fifty years from now we will look back on the times we are living in now and wonder what the fuck went wrong—guaranteed. The ringing of my work phone disturbs my thoughts. It's an Ohio number. Probably a distributor.

"This is Langston."

"Mr. Miller?"

"This is he," I answer in my work voice, which happens to be my every day voice also. I can hear the shuffling of papers on the other end. A country radio station, not loud, but loud enough. It sounds like Garth Brooks crooning in the background

"Well, sir, this is Bill Sanderson, I'm just following up on your book orders from last week. The files you sent were formatted incorrectly. Either we can do it for you, for an extra cost of course, or you can resend it yourself. Makes me no difference," he added.

"How much extra will it be?" Even though I knew I would have to do it myself I still wanted to know the price. "You sound like a reasonable person and we have many more projects in the pipeline with you."

"Well maybe we can work something out, but these book covers are just a tad too much."

"What do you mean?" I knew what he meant or at least what he was getting at.

"You know how *they* are always showing off their bodies, as if advertising it for profit. You know what I mean, right?" He felt comfortable talking to me. "You don't see James Patterson or Nicholas Sparks putting half-naked white women on their covers, do you?" He had a point there, even though Patterson and Nicholas don't write the kind of material that would need a half-naked or sensual woman on the cover.

"I understand your point," I placated him, "but it's a different landscape, than say even five years ago."

"Don't get me wrong, Mr. Miller, I like scantily clad women too, but if you need that to sell your book—then how good of a writer are you, huh?"

The entire conversation was making me uncomfortable. I half-expected a representative from HR to slide my cubicle door open and hand me a pink slip. But this kind of conversation was commonplace in our industry. The debate about what sells a book was as old as the content of song lyrics.

"There are so many choices for readers these days, so some writers feel obligated to seduce your eyes before they enter your mind. It doesn't matter what's between the pages, if no one picks it up. It just gathers dust and no one makes any money. I know that's not what you want."

"I realize that, but most of these books are just garbage. You know I'm right." He said it as if there was an implicit understanding between us. I sensed there was more he wanted to say and he was just feeling me out to see how far he could go.

"I can't disagree with you, Mr. Sanderson. The quality of checks and balances in the industry has been slowly eroding. Shoddy work is now standard, where once everyone took pride in putting out a great product. Now it's more about just saying you have a book and making money, than it is about quality. But in the end, readers make the decision what sells and what doesn't." I felt a bit hypocritical talking about money, even though I had never taken any shortcuts to getting a book published.

"Out here in Mack South, Ohio, we don't get too many people who read," He was searching for the right words, "*African-American literature.*" The words sounded heavy in his mouth, as if it took great effort to get it out before he choked on it. It was probably the first time he said the word, African-American.

"Well, that's good news in a way."

"How's that good news?"

"We are always looking for new demographics, new places to break out our writers."

He chuckled on the other end. He was probably trying to imagine his friends reading a popular urban book with a big booty woman, a gun or dollar bills plastered all over the cover.

"Mr. Sanderson, would you know of any local bookstores that would be interested in carrying some of our titles?"

"Well, I've lived here my entire life, Mr. Miller. Population is about six thousand. Most folks round here are church going people. I can tell you as assuredly as Hank Williams Sr. is singing *I Saw the Light* on the radio right now, that that kind of book will not sell one single copy in these parts."

I could have asked him if he didn't believe in the product then why print it. The answer was obvious and didn't need to be asked.

"Times are changing so maybe one day, a local bookstore will have a book signing for one our writers."

"Don't count on it anytime soon, Mr. Miller. Things are changing in Washington, DC where you are, but down here in Mack South, we're more on the traditional side."

"No one likes change but it's inevitable."

We chatted for a few more minutes about general things: sports, the weather, but I stayed away from politics.

"If you ever make it down this way to Mack South, Mr. Miller it would be my treat to take you out to one of our famous eateries, Cabana on the River. They can cook up you some of the biggest gulf shrimp you will ever see in your life. Alice will take great care of us. I think I might just head on over there for lunchtime and throw me back a few."

"We can call it a working lunch." Both of us laughed.

"If you don't mind me asking, Langston is an unusual name. How did you come about it?"

"My father is a big fan of the poet, Langston Hughes."

"That's different. Not too often you find a white man naming his son after a black writer."

That's when I should have said something and corrected his assumption. *I'm black.* Those two words would have made our otherwise pleasant conversation awkward. I didn't want to make him uncomfortable. I could almost hear my father's voice in head. *You need to make white folks feel uncomfortable, after all the shit they done put us through— it's the least you can do.* I am not my father. It wasn't the first time someone on the phone assumed I was white. My friends tease me sometimes and say I sound like Tiger Woods, all phony and shit. It's how I speak *all the time.* My mother was an English teacher. The only person allowed to speak bad English in our house was my dad. I think he did it on purpose sometimes just to irritate mother. *I can't speak proper all the time when this world is so messed up and trying to hold the black man down. My ancestors speak through me and this is the voice they understand.* Mother would scold him, but he would smile and kiss her, and before long they were laughing like two teenagers in love, even after forty-five years of marriage. Father didn't take no mess from anyone, no matter how many jobs it cost him. Mother understood his desire to be a man in a world that wasn't always fair, so she always supported his decisions. I could have corrected Mr. Sanderson, but there is a time and a place for everything. My father of course, would disagree. *Ain't no time like the present,* he would always say. *You might be dead later, so speak your truth now.*

6

MOST TIMES DREAMS and expectations don't match the results in the book industry. The cemetery of literary hopes and dreams is littered with discarded and unread books that someone put their heart and soul into, but the public didn't give a crap. In about an hour, I am supposed to email my list of writers their monthly royalty payments, before it hits their bank account tomorrow. Five minutes after I hit the SEND button, my phone and email will instantly blowup. I will have to patiently explain to them why they made less than an hourly worker at McDonalds. Books don't sell themselves; I will have to say for the thousandth time. Then they will say—what the hell do I have you for? We will go back and forth. Profanities from them, will assault my ears. I might even mute them a few times, scroll through a few Facebook pages, come back and they will still be ranting.

A lot of writers are like spoiled children, they demand things without understanding that it takes hard work to achieve your goal. So by this time, they have huffed and puffed and haven't gotten anywhere, so now it's my turn to speak. I explain to them once again that publishing isn't a get rich quick pyramid scheme. If no one is buying your paperback or downloading your EBooks, then that means no money is being generated. I continue by asking them how are they are marketing their books. Are they just doing online marketing, or calling up bookstores, local radio stations, trying to contact book clubs, doing free giveaways to entice readers they pick up their other titles? The answer generally is that they are too busy working on their next book. Most self-published writers don't want to hear the truth. The truth might make them give up. Truth is if a self-published book sells two hundred and fifty copies, then it's a moderate success. Writers get fooled into believing that everyone on their social media page will buy their books. If you have five thousand people on your page, and say, a hundred buy your book, then you are ahead of the game. Getting writers to understand that there's no correlation to their Facebook and Instagram likes and comments and their book sales is a job in itself.

The phone rings again and the caller starts to ramble on before I can get a word in.

"Miller—this here is some bullshit! What the fuck am I supposed to do with this piece of shit royalty check? I can't even buy a fucking meal at McDonalds. Somebody down there has my motherfucking money—and I aim to get what's mine motherfucker!"

Threats of bodily harm are just as common as badly edited

books in the world of self-publishing. This guy wasn't a gangsta, so I wasn't too concerned. His urban gangsta novels were almost laughable to read, even though he took his writing seriously. There was almost no chance he would ever make any money writing in that genre. His real name was Marvin Daniels and he wrote under the pseudonym, Lethal X. He had achieved moderate success a few years ago writing erotica novels, but had been unable to get signed to a major publishing company. The various cliques of book clubs and reader driven Facebook pages already had their allotted list of writers they were willing to support, so he decided to try his pen in street literature. The proliferation of writers in this genre exploring the same topics made me cringe as I strolled through Facebook pages. Most of them were pathetically predictable. You could basically look at the cover and predict the outcome of the book. Drug dealer seeks vengeance on his home boys. Young girl raped and now out for vengeance. Thug from neighborhood becomes kingpin of neighborhood. Rival gangs battle for turf and throw in the obligatory hot chick for further conflict. If the cover tells me the story, why do I need to read the book?

"Marvin-"

"The name is Lethal X."

"Okay, Lethal X how many eBooks do you think you sold last month?"

"At least a few hundreds. My fans on my page are going

crazy for the new book. You saw all those likes and comments the cover got, man?"

Likes and comments are not sales. They are ego stroking invisible hand jobs by anonymous people who forget who you are by the time they move on to the next status. If the majority of writers waited for their likes and comments to turn into actual book sales, they would starve to death and be homeless. There is a traffic jam on the literary highway and most of the product belongs in a junk yard. There is something nostalgic, magical about seeing something you wrote in print. For that reason alone, the badly written books will keep on coming. My hope is to find a few hidden gems when no one is looking. "We went over this last month. I checked out your page and there is always activity. You post excerpts; do giveaways, reader questions and celebrity news to interact with your fans, which are great, but your readers are not turning their enthusiasm for your posts into book sales. Once they leave your page, they forget who you are. You have to stalk them. Stay in contact, so they fall asleep with you on their mind and remember you when it's time to buy a book."

My words hit him hard. There was silence on the other end for about thirty seconds. I heard the faint sounds of a baby crying and Tom Joyner's laughter in the background. I had never met him face to face. We emailed. Spoke on the phone and skyped, which is as real as you can get these days. Not everyone's passion should be their career. Your passion doesn't always love you back. It's like falling in love with the wrong person. It's all a gamble. Against my advice, Marvin had quit his 9 to 5 job and decided that a real writer should believe in himself, despite the fact that many writers need a full-time job, just to pay the bills. His wife was none too pleased and had voiced her anger to me in a strongly, poorly written email, filled with grammatical errors, but she made her point by overusing her *fuck you's* and the obligatory asshole in every paragraph. My eyes hurt reading that email, but I kept it filed away in a folder in case I might need it for a book project later on. Maybe my memoirs.

His voice was soft now when he spoke. "Mr. Miller what am I going to do? I have a mortgage, kids, car note, school loans—what the hell was I thinking?" There were tears in his voice, even though he wasn't crying.

Reminding him that I had warned him against quitting his job would just be mean, but I had cautioned him to keep working and writing. Only mostly white writers had made it to Oprah, unless you're black and you have a celebrity profile, then maybe you stood a chance. The rest of them have to do it the old-fashioned way, as they hope to go viral and catch a wave of mass appeal.

"It will work out?" I tried to stay positive for his sake.

I was multi-tasking, still scrolling through Twitter, Instagram and Facebook pages as he droned on. A story on theroot.com about an unarmed black man being shot didn't hold my attention. I kept scrolling without stopping. Another story in Texas and New York about racial profiling made me scroll faster. Finally I clicked on a story that captures the interest of most people on the internet, something innocuous about a reality show and another one about Kim Kardashian's ass. The debate among the well-read was intense and swift. I read the comments without leaving my mark that I had ever been there.

7

AS USUAL I am the first one in the conference room for our weekly meeting about sales, signing new writers and anything else that was topical. I am big on appearances and made sure to be at meetings at least fifteen minutes before the start time. More employees strolled in late and took their seats without offering an apology. A man who is always late either doesn't care about his job and has no respect for his boss, my father always told us. My father's wisdom should have been a plus in the workforce, but he never rose higher than his politics would allow him to. He had never mastered the necessary skills of ass kissing and small talk, both necessary tools in stroking the egos of your immediate superiors. So he stayed in his place, because he didn't know his place which was just how he liked it.

The seats were set in a circle with the CEO, Mr. Bradford standing in the middle of it, directing the meeting. He said he preferred this style instead of sitting down because it allowed him to soak in the energy of his employees. I think he was probably a frustrated actor and he enjoyed the theater of having all eyes on him. He would swivel around, quite dramatically, as if he were some third rate entertainer in Las Vegas. No one laughed. He was the boss. My first week on the job, at the first meeting, he broke into his routine and I stood up to applaud, clapping my hands enthusiastically. No one else stood up. I sheepishly sat down, too late and the meeting continued. If I were white, my face would be the color of strawberries. A few co-workers razzed me after the meeting. It was their version of hazing. The CEO even laughed it off afterwards as we stood around chatting about the industry. I wanted to apologize, but apologizing would only make me look bad, so I kept quiet. The next time he did it, no one reacted and I did the same.

A hand patted my left shoulder and one of the agents sat down in the seat right next to me, even though the room was empty. I don't like men sitting that close to me. I am not homophobic, just uncomfortable with having to look at people who are right in my face space. His body was saturated in cologne and it stung my nose, but I kept a placid smile on my face. I hope it didn't look angry or resembled a smirk. I had practiced relaxing the muscles in my face to make me look calmer.

"He only notices when you're late. Other than that, he doesn't give a shit, really."

"So no brownie points, huh?"

"I've been here five years this December. If the boss was giving out brownie points, I would have collected a bagful my first few months here."

That's Richard Willis. A well-meaning middle age white dude, who was once a manager, but he had a big screw up from what I heard, and was lucky to keep his job. He's the kind of white dude who is unassuming and the minute you walk past him you forget you ever met him. People around here pretend that he doesn't even exist. In some ways, it's almost as if he were black, walking around invisible in plain view.

"Sign any new talent lately?"

His fat face turned sour at my innocent question. Sweat trickled down the side of his face. Either he didn't feel it or didn't care.

"Talent, huh, that's what you call it. Half the time it feels like I'm mining high school English classes for the bottom of the barrel writers, who think they're the next Salinger or Hemingway."

"You don't think any of your writers can have a best seller?"

"Sure. An Amazon best seller which can be manipulated because of the algorithms. New York Times best seller, well, that's more or less a pipe dream for most of the writers we represent. They believe it, so I don't encourage or dissuade it. It keeps them hoping. And what is life if there is no hope?"

"Do you really think that none of them will ever break through? You know it just takes something to go viral and then you ride the wave of mass appeal to become the next EL James."

He seemed to ponder what I had just said as he sipped on his *World's Greatest Dad* mug. I wondered if anyone had a *World's Shittiest Dad* mug somewhere. His grubby fingernails needed a manicure. The brown suit he wore hung loosely on his pudgy body, but he wasn't someone who was concerned with his appearance. A man like him had the concerns of family, a mortgage and trying to make sure some new hotshot didn't phase him out of a job.

"Does it bother you being the only black guy here?"

His question came out of the blue, but then I suppose questions like that are never just casual. There was some thought put into it before it left his mouth.

"We like to be called African-Americans now," I said jokingly.

"Being called African-American or black doesn't make your life any easier does it? At the end of the day the world views you the same, right?"

I wondered if he had ever had this kind of discussion with his friends or just me being the first black guy to work here, presented him with the opportunity to ask these questions. He stared at me, calmly, waiting for an answer. You always imagine having an answer these kinds of questions, but when it actually happens, your words cannot seem to find their out of your mind and into your mouth. It's only afterwards as you lay in bed hours later, a la George Costanza does the perfect response come to you.

"I hate to sound all Martin Lutherish, but I want to be judged by the content of my character and not this," I touched my hand and watched his hand which was on the table next to mine. The different shades of our hands made me think of a museum piece on race relations. Two guys walked in fiddling with their Android and iPhones. They sat down without saying anything and continued playing with their gadgets, oblivious to both of us sitting there.

"The world does not work that way, my friend. In business there is no true altruism. Everything is done with the bottom line in mind. We are just dollars on a chess board." He nodded at me as if we had an understanding, a shared secret. He stared straight ahead, tapping his fingers against the brown table surface, but he remained quiet.

The room is now filled with employees chatting about their latest projects. Richard has other things on his mind, so I am left sitting, alone and having to appear as if I am cool with that. You can only stare at your phone for so long, with your head down, before you lift your eyes to see if anyone has noticed how uncomfortable you are. Finally the CEO made his grand entrance. I wondered if he had a flunky who alerted him as to when the room was sufficiently filled, so all eyes would be on him. It takes a special kind of person to be a CEO of a company. A sprinkle of narcissism is needed   to believe that only you can lead an entire company to the Promised Land.

"Let's get down to business." He strides directly to the middle of the circle. Sitting down, he seems taller as he towers over everyone. Maybe that was the intent of his entire shtick or maybe something he learned at a management seminar. "Before I continue with business this is our first company meeting since Langston Miller joined our little firm. I'm still not sure why he chose us," he winks at me dramatically, "but we are happy to have him here with us. Great things are expected. Anything you need let me know and I will make it happen. Any new clients?" He asked hopefully.

There is nothing like your boss offering you up in front of everyone as if you are some sort of savior. It puts the spotlight on you and by the time this meeting is over, my name will have been searched on Google countless times, anonymous friend requests from co-workers looking to rifle through my friend lists for possible clients. I know they will do it, because it's what I did at my previous job when the new guy was hired.

I imagined an assortment of blue and brown eyes on me, awaiting a response from the new black guy. Even when you shouldn't feel that way, it always seems as if you are an ambassador for your race. You carry a certain responsibility to act right, to do better, so the next person in the door doesn't have to wear that weight. But the next person doesn't always know that the road has been somewhat paved for them, so the terrain is easier to maneuver. There isn't a database network to log into to keep each other abreast of the work that's being done. Just know that whatever door you walk through, someone left their footprints there for you to follow. There were invisible eyes on me from the past and the future, and the ever present voice of my father in my ears, telling me much is expected of me. I expect more of myself than he could ever expect of me.

"I have a few promising leads. I plan on closing a few of them shortly," I added confidently. I didn't want to sound too cocky, so I quickly added, "I'm glad to be here on this team and look forward to learning from everyone here." Even when you don't mean these things at work, you say it, so your co-workers won't hate your ass. I was used to being the odd man out. The new black guy on the scene. Everyone smiles at you. You smile back and make nice. Behind the polite banter and questions is the search for answers. Smart people let you reveal who you are without you even realizing they have created a profile on you, without even having to pay for it online.

"That's what I like to hear," he spins around to face a few employees seated behind him. "Be careful my friends, Langston might be the one getting that 10k bonus this year. He might just outwork all of you."

No one said a word. Tight smiles. Smirks. Their confidence still intact. I could see they didn't think I had what it took. It didn't matter that I was the first one here every morning and the last to leave. I never went to Happy Hour or took part in any social gatherings. I was always all business all the time.

"Okay, let's get down to business. You need to push the Gold Package more to your new writers. The Standard Package isn't enough to get them where they want to be. That's what you tell them. In order to compete with the big publishing houses, they need the GP. The GP gets them eyes. Without eyes, they might as well be blind."

I wanted to ask him if any writers who bought the GP package had experienced any marked increase in sales. It was a valid question, but the new guy never puts the CEO on the spot. It wouldn't be hard to check the database to find out. Simply looking at Amazon's Top 100 books in various genres would tell me what I needed to know.

Nathan covered a few more issues. Took a few questions. I listened and sized up my co-workers. The usual banter flowed around the room about the industry. E-book pricing. The war between Amazon and Hachette Publishing. The room was split as to who would win that fight. Amazon was viewed by most as the big, bad bully on the block, crushing everything in its way, but the bully had grown so strong over the years, that taking it on now was tantamount to writing your own eulogy. When the bully is giving you discounts and giving you such good service that no one else can rival it, you begin to fall in love with the bully, even when you know that the bully is trying to crush everyone around it, so it can control your mind.

"See you around," Richard said as he strolled away. He didn't engage anyone in conversation and quickly disappeared through the swinging doors.

"That old man is out to pasture. It's a new age and he hasn't caught up yet. He still has a fucking flip phone. Can you believe that shit?"

The voice came from across the room. It was Mr. IPhone. It wasn't Friday but he was dressed like it was a dress down day. Jeans. Sneakers. A faded yellow t-shirt that read: KINDLE ME! His face looked sunburned, as if he had just returned from vacation. It wouldn't be long until it returned to its natural color. Tattoos adorned his arms and neck, but he didn't look dangerous. He seemed to be more like the type of guy who was into the latest fashion trend and there was no real commitment on his part to whatever he was advertising. He was just living the life and along for the ride. He was a poser.

"He seems okay."

His eyes are still glued to his iPhone as his long fingers glides over the smooth surface. I wondered if he was texting about me or just surfing the internet.

"I bet you the old man didn't tell you that Nathan transferred most of his clients to you, right?"

"It never came up, but I'm sure there's a good reason.

Maybe he had too many and Nathan was just freeing him up for some other stuff."

Calling my boss by his first name didn't feel right, even though he wasn't in the room. I have a thing about calling my elders by their appropriate title. It keeps everyone in their right place and the world moves smoothly along.

"Richard was in charge of the Black Writers." He finally looks up from his phone to stare at me. "Excuse me, *African-American* writers. But a few of them complained that they thought a *brother,*" the word sounded distasteful on his tongue and seemed to spit from his lips, "would have more of a vested interest in their success which is ridiculous." I imagined him using another word to describe us among his friends. When I was a kid, my friends and I took great pleasure in saying the word, fuck. We weren't allowed to say it, but it made us feel powerful, grownup to say it among ourselves. I imagine that's how some white folks who say nigger feel when they are in private. They inherently know it's wrong, but just saying it, is like giving the middle finger to the world and the people they believe are trying to control what they say.

He was baiting me. The angry black man inside of me debated whether or not to engage. Engaging had real world consequences. Staying docile had deeper implications for me as a black man. Being black in America or most places these days is like constantly walking a tightrope. The slightest deviation from your routine can lead to your demise. The things we have to deal with on a daily basis, white people will never understand the level of restraint it takes to live in this world, in this skin, daily, and not express the rage we sometimes feel at the constant injustices and humiliations we have to endure.

His buzz cut didn't fit his angular face. It looked like pubic hair cut too short. He had watched one too many movies. His stare reminded me of Christian Bale in Batman. He even sounded like him, down to the gravelly voice of death. All I had to do was cast my line to catch what he wanted to tell me. I don't like confrontation. It is not my nature. I would rather talk than get loud or use my fists. Sometimes a man has no choice but to use his fists to get his words to make sense, that's my father again getting all Malcolm X on me. One day you will access your rage. Rage you never thought you were capable of, he would say to me. It's not the sixties Pops, I would respond. They don't seem to know that was always his response.

Unarmed Black Men
Killed by Police from 2015-2018

Artago Damon Howard

Jeremy Lett

Lavall Hall

Thomas Allen

Charly Leundeu Keunang

Naeschylus Vinzant

Tony Robinson

Anthony Hill

Bobby Gross

Brandon Jones

Eric Harris

Walter Scott

Frank Shephard

William Chapman

David Felix

Brendon Glenn

Kris Jackson

Spencer McCain

Victor Emanuel Larosa

Salvado Ellswood

Albert Joseph Davis

Darrius Stewart

Samuel DuBose

Michael Eugene Wilson Jr.

Christian Taylor

Asshams Pharoah Manley

Felix Kumi

India Kager

Keith Harrison McLeod

Junior Prosper

Anthony Ashford

Bennie Lee Tignor

Jamar Clark

Nathaniel Harris Pickett

Miguel Espinal

Michael Noel

Kevin Matthews

Bettie Jones

Keith Childress

Antronie Scott

David Joseph

Calin Roquemore

Dyzhawn L. Perkins

Christopher J. Davis

Peter Gaines

Kevin Hicks

Jessica Nelson-Williams

Vernell Bing

Antwun Shumpert
Deravis Caine Rogers
Dalvin Hollins
Donnell Thompson
Levonia Riggins
Terence Crutcher
Alfred Olango
Christopher Sowell
Andrew Depeiza
JR Williams
Darrion Barnhill
Nana Adomako
Chad Robertson
Raynard Burton
Alteria Woods
Jordan Edwards
Ricco Devante Holden
Marc Brandon Davis
David Jones
Aaron Bailey
Dejuan Guillory
Brian Easley
Isaiah Tucker

Charles David Robinson
Anthony Antonio Ford
Dewboy Lister
Calvin Toney
Lawrence Hawkins
Keita O'Neil
Jean Pedro Pierre
Arther McAfee Jr.
Ronnell Foster
Shermichael Ezeff
Cameron Hall
Stephon Clark
Danny Thomas
Juan Markee Jones
Marcus-David L. Peters
Robert Lawrence White
Antwon Rose
Anthony Marcell Green
Rashaun Washington
Cynthia Fields
Charles Roundtree
Jesse J. Quinton
TK TK

Source: The Washington Post Online Database

Paperbacks available @ <u>www.deanjeanpierre.com</u> & KINDLE

Woman Worship 4

Rage

The Killer In You

Orgasms for Lunch (E-book)

Birthday Girl Dessert (E-book)

A Killer Review (E-book)

I Didn't Mean to Kill My Neighbor (E-book)

Crave

The Randomness of Everything

Don't Mess With Eva

The Killing Club of Ex-Girlfriends

Kiss Me Softly

Woman Worship 3

Insatiable (1-2)

Assume The Position

Woman Worship 2

Stiff (E-book)

Moist

Aural Sex (Poetry CD)

Cum For Me

Woman Worship

The Pussy Whispers

www.ingramcontent.com/pod-product-compliance
Lightning Source LLC
LaVergne TN
LVHW041220080426
835508LV00011B/1011